RAND ARROYO CENTER

T0302891

Pacific Engagement

Forging Tighter Connections
Between Tactical Security Cooperation
Activities and U.S. Strategic Goals in
the Asia-Pacific Region

Stephen Watts, Christopher M. Schnaubelt, Sean Mann,
Angela O'Mahony, Michael Schwille

Prepared for the United States Army

For more information on this publication, visit www.rand.org/t/RR1920

Library of Congress Cataloging-in-Publication Data is available for this publication.
ISBN: 978-0-8330-9813-9

Published by the RAND Corporation, Santa Monica, Calif.
© Copyright 2018 RAND Corporation
RAND® is a registered trademark.

Support RAND
Make a tax-deductible charitable contribution at
www.rand.org/giving/contribute

www.rand.org

Preface

This report documents research and analysis conducted as part of a project entitled *Meeting Engagement Demands with Army Forces*, co-sponsored by I Corps and U.S. Army Pacific (USARPAC). The purpose of the project was to better align tactical-level activities with strategic goals by improving processes for planning, coordination, and evaluation. The project analyzed U.S. Army processes for security cooperation at the strategic, operational, and tactical levels, with a focus on the U.S. Pacific Command area of responsibility. Although the research focused specifically on USARPAC, I Corps, and subordinate commands, the results are likely to be of interest to a broad range of professionals who are involved in the planning and execution of security cooperation.

The Project Unique Identification Code (PUIC) for the project that produced this document is HQD156912.

This research was conducted within RAND Arroyo Center's Strategy, Doctrine, and Resources Program. RAND Arroyo Center, part of the RAND Corporation, is a federally funded research and development center (FFRDC) sponsored by the United States Army.

RAND operates under a "Federal-Wide Assurance" (FWA00003425) and complies with the Code of Federal Regulations for the Protection of Human Subjects Under United States Law (45 CFR 46), also known as "the Common Rule," as well as with the implementation guidance set forth in DoD Instruction 3216.02. As applicable, this compliance includes reviews and approvals by RAND's Institutional Review Board (the Human Subjects Protection Committee) and by the U.S. Army. The views of sources utilized in this study are solely their own and do not represent the official policy or position of DoD or the U.S. Government.

Contents

Figures

Tables

Summary

This report examines U.S. Army security cooperation (SC) processes in the U.S. Pacific Command (USPACOM) area of responsibility (AOR). The goal of the report is to forge a better link between strategic and tactical levels in the planning and execution of SC activities so as to achieve the United States' shaping goals in the theater. More specifically, this report seeks to accomplish the following goals:

- Develop a framework to link tactical- and operational-level SC activities with strategic goals.
- Identify information requirements for units executing SC activities.
- Identify ways to improve evaluations.
- Propose options for improving the quality, timeliness, and effectiveness of information flows between strategic and tactical levels involved in SC.

Our Research Methods

The research team sought to understand better what works well in theater SC processes and what could be improved through several types of analysis. The team completed the following research tasks:

- a review of applicable U.S. military doctrine
- an analysis of military orders and other guidance for SC activities in the Asia-Pacific region

- a review of after-action reports and other documents and databases assessing the conduct and effectiveness of U.S. activities
- interviews with U.S. military personnel at nearly every echelon involved in these activities.

All data for this report was collected by January 2016.

What We Found

Our research on SC processes was divided into two primary areas: planning and evaluation. Coordination issues were generally associated with one of these primary areas. Overall, we found that U.S. Army SC processes in this theater generally function at least adequately and often well. However, processes might be improved in a number of areas.

Planning

Planning and executing an SC event requires extensive coordination on the part of U.S. Army Pacific (USARPAC), I Corps, and executing units. The existing coordination system is built on the formal orders chain, multiechelon planning conferences, and other direct communications. This system generally functions well, though challenges remain. These include turnover and personnel shortfalls, as well as processes that do not adequately ensure that the right information gets to the right people.

Several of the coordination problems identified by interviewees were caused by inconsistent adherence to established practice, rather than problems with the system itself. Some of these departures from standard practice appear rooted in growing pains associated with recent changes that reassigned responsibility for many SC event management tasks from USARPAC to I Corps.[1] Both USARPAC and I Corps have

---

[1]   As part of the rebalance to the Asia-Pacific, both USARPAC and I Corps have undertaken new responsibilities. USARPAC is now a four-star headquarters, with responsibilities exclusively at the strategic level. Many of the operational responsibilities that previously resided with USARPAC are now being devolved to I Corps. At the same time, I Corps has gained a broader span of control, becoming the operational-level headquarters for nearly all

new opportunities to reassess the procedures by which they plan, coordinate, and evaluate SC.

USARPAC and I Corps are aware of and have addressed some of these issues already. Some remaining challenges might be addressed through improved communications practices. Multiechelon involvement in planning conferences, for instance, is an extremely useful practice that should be sustained. However, these conferences seldom result in an authoritative record of what was decided. The absence of such a summary document can create situations in which different planners have different interpretations of what was decided at these events. Such divergences seem particularly common due to personnel turnover. Routine turnover in corps and division staff, as well as planning and event execution leaders at the brigade and battalion level, mean that the personnel in charge of event execution may not have attended the planning conferences.

USARPAC generally issues orders for SC events sufficiently far ahead of the actual events that tactical-level planners can adequately plan for them. The exceptions appeared to be cases in which a short-notice event was driven by requirements external to USARPAC, such as a quick turnaround request from a partner nation passed through a country team. Interview respondents acknowledged that broad orders covering multiple large events could be issued up to a year ahead of time, which would enable tactical-level units to begin planning for events, even if many of the specifics of the events would be filled in over the course of the year.

Orders for SC events generally provided detailed information related to technical military and logistics concerns. They rarely provided detailed information about the broader strategic goals of an SC event; prior SC activities with the partner and how the present event built on these prior activities; or the capabilities or challenges of partner-nation forces. Tactical-level planners can potentially obtain much or all

---

Army units aligned to the USPACOM AOR. (The "rebalance" was articulated in a series of speeches by then–President Barack Obama and other major announcements. See White House Office of the Press Secretary, "Remarks by President Obama to the Australian Parliament," November 17, 2011.)

of this information from other sources, but it was not clear that they always did so. Numerous interview subjects mentioned that the origins of these events were often obscure. Providing planners with executive summaries of the meetings in which these events were proposed and planned would help establish SC events' broader strategic context.

While information on strategic goals and context can potentially be found in a variety of sources, none of these sources offers authoritative guidance. We found that many orders provide only vague guidance about the broader objectives of an event and how to prioritize these various objectives. Several interview subjects reported that different tactical-level planners could therefore interpret guidance very differently, sometimes leading to friction between various elements. Greater specificity in orders would likely help to ensure that the commander's intent is realized and all elements have a common understanding of event objectives and priorities.

Finally, the research team identified a number of challenges related to staffing, resources, and business practices (especially those involving passports). Most of these challenges require support from outside entities, such as the State Department, or additional resources. Additional resources could help improve knowledge management to fix high-impact shortfalls in communicating key information to the correct echelons and increase the number of planners at the corps level to match the increase in exercise planning responsibilities.

Evaluation

Our analysis of USARPAC's evaluation procedures found that although many of the components necessary for integrating evaluation into each step of the SC decision cycle are in place, critical information is missing. USARPAC's evaluation process breaks down in two key places. First, at a conceptual level, USARPAC's strategic evaluation process often does a poor job of specifying precise links between tactical activities and strategic objectives. Second, much of the data necessary to make informed evaluations are not currently being collected. Tactical-level units could help to fill this gap. A combination of better data collection and management could increase the quality and quantity of information available to operational and strategic planners. Our recommendations include designating or creating a widely accessible information portal; additional suggested tools are included in the appendixes.

Strategic evaluation enables USARPAC to ascertain whether its SC activities have helped to accomplish its strategic objectives; update its set of SC activities in light of lessons learned and progress toward its strategic objectives; and provide feedback and guidance to tactical units to execute their SC-related missions. USARPAC's strategic evaluation process is based on three main components: (1) professional judgment from line of effort (LOE) managers (senior officers responsible for evaluating USARPAC lines of effort); (2) country environmental assessments from the Political, Military, Economic, Social, Infrastructure, and Information (PMESII) framework;[2] and (3) assessments of how SC activities contribute to strategic objectives, using the Strategic Management System (SMS) framework. Of these three components, the LOE manager's judgment currently carries the most weight. The SMS framework is often ignored due to concerns over the quality of the framework's information.

Strengthening USARPAC's strategic evaluation process depends on improving the usefulness of the SMS framework. In particular, two key changes would strengthen strategic evaluation processes. A theories-of-change framework will help planners identify strategic effects, intermediate military objectives and SC activities, and the concomitant measures of effectiveness (MOEs) and measures of performance (MOPs) that are assumed to be causally linked to strategic objectives. Clearly specified theories of change will also help evaluators to identify when hypothesized causal relationships received support through the collected MOEs and MOPs. For SC activities that are strategically important, entail causal relationships that are conceptually uncertain, and are conducted with partners committed to working with the United States, USARPAC could also implement impact evaluations to test specific propositions more rigorously.

At the tactical level, evaluation enables executing units to determine whether they have fulfilled their stated mission objectives, learned

---

[2] A PMESII framework is a standard military model for organizing data on an actor or environment.

from the event, and passed along that knowledge to other units. The process is conducted through an after-action review or after-action report (AAR). In our review of tactical-level evaluation, we found that critical information is missing from unit-level AARs. Even where this information was present, knowledge management practices made it difficult to access. Units should focus on improving the quality of information they provide to ensure that it is relevant for planners and evaluators, working with partner-nation security forces to help establish a baseline of knowledge for individual units, and ensuring that AARs are submitted and stored in the appropriate repository that is accessible to all.

What We Recommend

This report recommends ten changes to SC planning processes in theater.

USARPAC should do the following:

- Adopt "theories of change"—a framework widely used in the development community—as a part of the planning process.
- Better incorporate tactical-level information into USARPAC's strategic evaluation process.
- Create accessible country folders with details on logistics and other requirements. Information technology and knowledge management barriers currently prevent many potential users from accessing what information is currently available.
- Consider requesting a State Department waiver to enable the issuance of official passports without providing a travel manifest, similar to the U.S. Government Accountability Office (GAO) recommendation regarding U.S. Africa Command.[3]
- Consider issuing guidance that clarifies the prioritization and interrelationship between unit readiness and SC objectives.

---

[3]   GAO, "Regionally Aligned Forces: DoD Could Enhance Army Brigades' Efforts in Africa by Improving Activity Coordination and Mission-Specific Preparation," GAO-15-568, August 2015.

USARPAC and I Corps should do the following:
- Improve subordinate units' access to cultural information.
- Provide additional information to "neck down" strategic guidance to tactical objectives and help units execute in line with commander's intent.
- All echelons should sustain the current best practice of multiechelon involvement in planning conferences, Operational Planning Teams, etc.
- Improve access and create standardized portal(s) with logistics and business practice guidance for each partner nation, with a clear lead responsible for updating guidance and answering questions.
- Should resourcing become available, prioritize major subordinate command staffs for additional personnel to support planning.

The report recommends several additional changes to the way that evaluations are conducted.

USARPAC should do the following:

- Consider adopting a theory-of-change approach to improve conceptual clarity. As part of that effort, USARPAC should update the (often implicit) causal assumptions in its current SMS framework.
- Develop MOEs and MOPs that more appropriately reflect USARPAC's intermediate military objectives and tasks.
- Evaluate whether the PMESII framework includes the right information to assess the impact of external factors on USARPAC SC activities.
- Consider supplementing the current strategic evaluation process with impact evaluations that use rigorous methodologies to identify the extent to which programs and activities produced the desired effects.

I Corps and its subordinate commands should do the following:

- More fully use the knowledge management and evaluation tools already available, such as Global Theater Security Cooperation

Management Information System and USARPAC's existing information repositories.

- Work to improve the critical content of AARs, potentially using any one of a number of well-established processes for facilitating such analyses.
- Focus on improving the quality of information they provide to ensure that it is relevant for planners and evaluators, working with partner-nation security forces to help establish a baseline of knowledge for individual units, and ensuring that AARs are submitted and stored in the appropriate repository that is accessible to all.
- To improve the quality, quantity, and accessibility of information in AARs, I Corps and subordinate commands should consider adopting AAR templates designed to elicit critical information from SC event participants.

Taken together, these recommendations offer opportunities to improve the flow of guidance and information between strategic and tactical levels, better linking specific SC activities to the strategic goals that they are intended to support. Given limited resources, the priority should be actions that improve knowledge management and operational-level staffing for planning requirements.

Acknowledgments

The authors are grateful first and foremost to the leadership and staff of I Corps and U.S. Army Pacific (USARPAC) for sponsoring and facilitating this research. LTG Stephen Lanza and MG William Fuller of I Corps and Maj. Gen. Gregory Bilton and MG Todd McCaffrey of USARPAC helped to launch the research and provided invaluable feedback. COL Jeffrey Klein, COL Newman Yang, and John M. Waite oversaw the project for USARPAC and provided valuable insights; we are particularly grateful to Waite for his help in facilitating meetings with USARPAC and U.S. Pacific Command (USPACOM) personnel and providing documents and data on USARPAC planning and operations. On the I Corps side, COL David Danikowski, COL Timothy King, and LTC Krivda provided oversight at various points, while MAJ Joseph Gainey, MAJ Jason Dye, and MAJ Kari Lewis were extremely helpful in rounding up documents and arranging meetings. As the I Corps liaison to USARPAC, LTC Scott Peachey provided invaluable data and insights that helped us to understand the links between the two commands.

The authors also owe a debt to the dozens of U.S. government personnel who took the time to speak with us about their roles and observations related to security cooperation in the Asia-Pacific. We conducted all of our interviews on a not-for-attribution basis, so we cannot identify our interviewees by name. If they read this report, though, we hope they will recognize their contributions to our findings. Without their support, this research would not have been possible.

We are also grateful to a number of others for their insights and critical feedback on our research. LTC Dan Gibson played a critical role in the early days of this project as a U.S. Army Fellow at RAND; our research was greatly improved by his participation. Chris Nelson and Bill Gelfeld generously shared their time and insights from their prior research. We are grateful to Chris Pernin, Mike Mazarr, and Wade Markel for their comments and suggestions throughout the project. Reviewers Jennifer Moroney and David Maxwell asked thoughtful questions and made sure we adequately explained our methods. Jerry Sollinger provided invaluable assistance to improve the presentation of the findings and recommendations. Finally, we are thankful to Natalie Kauppi and Jessica Wolpert for their expert assistance in formatting and preparing this report for final submission.

Abbreviations

25ID	25th Infantry Division
AAR	after-action report
ADP	Army Doctrine Publication
ADRP	Army Doctrinal Reference Publication
AOR	area of responsibility
ARNORTH	Army North
ASCC	Army service component command
CALL	Center for Army Lessons Learned
CCMR	Center for Civil-Military Relations
CG	commanding general
CSCP	Country Security Cooperation Plan
DoD	Department of Defense
DRU	direct reporting unit
ERP	Engagement Resource Plan
ESB	Executive Steering Board
FM	Field Manual
FMS	foreign military sales

FRAGO	fragmentary order
FSF	foreign security forces
FXD-SCP	Strategic Effects Directorate – Security Cooperation and Policy
FY	fiscal year
GAO	U.S. Government Accountability Office
GEF	Guidance for Employment of the Force
G-TSCMIS	Global Theater Security Cooperation Management Information System
IT	information technology
JP	Joint Publication
JSCP	Joint Strategic Capabilities Plan
LOA	letter of authorization
LOE	line of effort
LOO	line of operation
MOE	measure of effectiveness
MOP	measure of performance
NMC	National Military Strategy
OAA	operations, actions, and activities
OPORD	operational order
PMESII	Political, Military, Economic, Social, Infrastructure, and Information
RSOI	reception, staging, onward movement, and integration
SC	security cooperation

SME	subject-matter expert
SMS	Strategic Management System
TCP	Theater Campaign Plan
TCSP	Theater Campaign Support Plan
TSC	Theater Security Cooperation
TSCO	Theater Support Campaign Order
TSCP	Theater Security Cooperation Plan
USAFRICOM	U.S. Africa Command
USARPAC	U.S. Army, Pacific
USPACOM	U.S. Pacific Command
WARNO	warning order
WMD	weapon of mass destruction

CHAPTER ONE

Introduction

Background

The United States participates in hundreds of cooperative activities with partner nations throughout the world every year. These peacetime activities—known collectively as security cooperation (SC)—refer to

> All Department of Defense interactions with foreign defense establishments to build defense relationships that promote specific U.S. security interests, develop allied and friendly military capabilities for self-defense and multinational operations, and provide U.S. forces with peacetime and contingency access to a host nation.[1]

The United States conducts these events with two purposes. First, participation in these events helps to improve U.S. military unit readiness; forces that operate in unfamiliar terrain and cooperate with foreign military personnel are likely to be better prepared the next time they deploy for an overseas contingency. Second, the United States pursues these activities to help shape the theaters in which U.S. forces operate. Specifically, SC events should forge strong relationships with U.S. partners, help develop partners' military capabilities and ability to operate with U.S. forces, and facilitate access to foreign countries in the event of a contingency.[2]

---

[1] Joint Publication (JP) 1-02, *DoD Dictionary of Military and Associated Terms*, Washington, D.C.: Department of Defense, November 8, 2010, as amended through February 15, 2016, p. 212.

[2] Field Manual (FM) 3-22, *Army Support to Security Cooperation*, Washington, D.C., Headquarters, Department of the Army, January 2013, p. 1-1.

The readiness goals of SC events are relatively straightforward; preparing for and executing military operations is what military units do. The shaping goals of SC, on the other hand, are much more complex.[3] The answers to many strategic-level questions remain unclear. Do such activities routinely help to build partners' capabilities? Does working closely together in a major exercise necessarily build stronger relationships, or could cultural misunderstandings or other frictions sometimes damage them? Under what conditions is SC most likely to succeed? How can planners know in advance when success is most likely? How should SC activities balance training U.S. units and building partner-nation capacity?

The complexities of these shaping goals are further magnified by the complexities of U.S. planning processes. Planning for large-scale SC events typically begins more than a year ahead of time. On the U.S. side, the concept for an event is typically developed by staff at U.S. embassies and at the headquarters of U.S. geographic combatant commands, such as U.S. Pacific Command (USPACOM), U.S. European Command, and U.S. Africa Command (USAFRICOM). Yet tactical-level unit leaders execute these plans, and they are far removed from where the strategic-level planning takes place. Large-scale events typically require dozens of planners, scattered across a variety of commands and embassies, to coordinate on a wide range of issues.

Given these enormous complexities, how can U.S. personnel responsible for SC events be certain that they are achieving their theater-shaping objectives? How can they ensure that key event leaders and planners are operating according to a common concept? And

---

[3]   Army doctrine describes a "decisive-shaping-sustaining framework" and states that "Shaping operations create and preserve conditions for the success of the decisive operation." (Army Doctrine Publication [ADP] 3-0, *Unified Land Operations*, Washington, D.C.: Headquarters, Department of the Army, October 2011, p. 13). The Army Strategic Guidance for Security Cooperation explains the linkage between security cooperation as a shaping activity and decisive operations: "security cooperation builds defense relationships that promote national security interests, develops allied and friendly military capabilities for self-defense and multinational operations, and provides Joint Forces with peacetime and contingency access" (John M. McHugh and Raymond T. Odierno, "Army Strategic Guidance for Security Cooperation: An Enduring Mission for Prevent, Shape, Win," Department of the Army, August 2014).

how can they be certain the concept is the right one for achieving U.S. strategic objectives?

Purpose

This report examines SC processes in the USPACOM area of responsibility (AOR) as executed by U.S. Army Pacific (USARPAC) and I Corps.[4] The goal of the report is to provide USARPAC and I Corps with a framework and tools to forge better links between strategic and tactical levels in the planning and execution of SC activities, identify key requirements for information, and suggest options to help USPACOM achieve the United States' shaping goals in the theater. More specifically, this report seeks to accomplish the following objectives related to USARPAC and I Corps SC activities:

- Develop a framework for linking tactical- and operational-level SC activities with strategic goals.
- Identify information requirements for units executing SC activities.
- Identify requirements for improved evaluations.
- Propose options for improving the quality, timeliness, and effectiveness of information flows between strategic and tactical levels involved in SC.

Approach

We used quantitative and qualitative methods to analyze the SC processes used by USARPAC and I Corps at the time of writing, draw conclusions about what was working well and what could be improved, and develop recommendations for improvement (or sustainment in the case of processes that were working well). Periodic in-process reviews

---

[4] U.S. Special Forces, as well as other special operations forces, perform a great deal of SC activities in the USPACOM AOR. However, since this report focuses upon processes within USARPAC and I Corps, we did not include them within the scope of this study.

with action officers designated by the sponsors ensured our study continued to meet the sponsors' objectives as we developed the research design and narrowed our focus to specific aspects of USARPAC and I Corps SC activities. All data for this report was collected by January 2016.

To inform our analysis, we began with a review of the relevant Department of Defense (DoD) and Army doctrinal publications, as well as various Government Accountability Office (GAO) reports and other literature related to SC in general and specifically in the USPACOM AOR.[5] Our review focused on determining the stated strategic goals and guidance on the design and execution of SC activities.

Afterward, we reviewed a total of 59 after-action reports (AARs) from a spectrum of SC engagements across the services, particularly from the Army and Marine Corps (see Figure 1.1), as they tend to perform similar types of SC activities (ground force operations).[6] Within this set of AARs, we found that most of the reported challenges related to:

- sufficiency of information and guidance conveyed from headquarters to executing units
- timeliness of missions assignment
- evaluation of SC event outcomes.

---

[5]   Relevant DoD and Army doctrinal publications included JP 5-0, *Joint Operation Planning*, Washington, D.C.: Joint Chiefs of Staff, August 11, 2011; ADP 5-0, *The Operations Process*, Washington, D.C.: Headquarters, Department of the Army, May 17, 2012; Department of the Army Pamphlet 11-31, *Army Security Cooperation Handbook*, Washington, D.C.: Headquarters, Department of the Army, February 6, 2015; and FM 3-07.1, *Security Force Assistance*, Washington, D.C.: Headquarters, Department of the Army, May 1, 2009.

[6]   The AARs covered five geographic combatant commands from a variety of sources, including the Center for Army Lessons Learned, the Joint Lessons Learned Information System, the Marine Corps Center for Lessons Learned, and the I Corps Knowledge Management page. Thirty of the AARs came from USPACOM, with 51 percent of those from the Army, 47 percent from the Marine Corps and 2 percent from the Air Force. AARs reviewed covered the years 2008 through 2015, with the majority coming from events held in 2014.

Figure 1.1
Summary of Issues Found in AARs

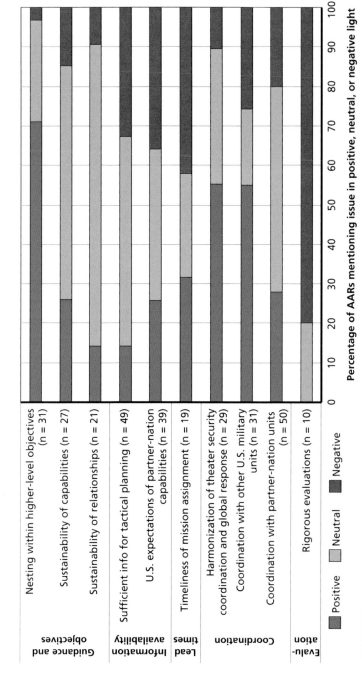

RAND RR1920-1.1

Based upon these findings, and with concurrence of the sponsor, we focused our interviews and examination of orders upon these aspects of SC planning and reporting processes.

Next, we conducted semistructured interviews with 57 soldiers and U.S. government civilians assigned to USARPAC and units at the corps level and below.[7] During these interviews, we asked interviewees to describe the SC activity planning process and provide their perceptions of which aspects of SC planning were going well and which could be improved. We also asked them to provide suggestions on improving the process.

These AAR reviews and interviews allowed us to perform process tracing to compare the planning process as prescribed with the "real-world" planning process.

We also reviewed a set of 42 orders for fiscal year (FY) 2015 Army SC events in the Pacific that involved both USARPAC and I Corps. These included all 23 FY 2015 USARPAC orders directing I Corps to carry out an SC activity outside of the United States. The remaining 19 orders, issued by I Corps or subordinate headquarters, were the only ones we were able to locate. Unlike the USARPAC orders, these do not represent an exhaustive dataset of all I Corps orders directing subordinates to carry out SC activities outside of the United States.[8] As discussed in the section on specific planning issues below, our analysis of these orders focused on lead times prior to activity execution (were orders issued in a timely manner?) and sufficiency of objective guidance and planning information (did orders contain the information necessary for subordinate headquarters to conduct effective planning?)[9]

---

[7]   These interviews were conducted on a not-for-attribution basis between November 2 and November 13, 2015, at Fort Shafter, Hawaii; the Asia-Pacific Center for Security Studies, Honolulu, Hawaii; and Joint Base Lewis-McChord, Washington. The echelons represented ranged from company commander to corps and theater Army G-staff, with ranks from E-7 to O-7. Although a few individual interviews were conducted, the majority were focus group sessions organized by unit or section.

[8]   The apparent absence of a full set of I Corps SC orders for FY 2015 is illustrative of the gaps in knowledge management that will be described later in this report.

[9]   For timeliness, we compared the number of days between the date that I Corps received an order from USARPAC and issuing an order to I Corps' subordinate units. For sufficiency

Finally, we weaved the results from process tracing, stakeholder perceptions, and analysis of orders to identify key chokepoints and gaps within the SC processes. These chokepoints and gaps were used to produce our findings. We used expert knowledge, including interaction with key stakeholders, to develop recommendations on addressing shortfalls and sustaining elements that we assessed as working well.

Organization of This Report

The remainder of this report is divided into three chapters. Chapter Two examines issues related to SC planning, including the processes for translating broad strategic goals into actionable tactical-level objectives, the availability of information required by tactical-level planners, and the timeliness of SC mission assignment. Chapter Three examines issues related to the evaluation of SC activities at both the strategic and tactical levels. Issues of coordination between strategic, operational, and tactical levels are addressed in both of these chapters. Chapter Four concludes with our recommendations.

---

of information, we used the AAR coding scheme shown in Appendix A of this report.

CHAPTER TWO

USARPAC and I Corps Roles in SC Planning

Introduction

Both USARPAC and I Corps play key roles in the complex, multi-layered planning processes that underlie SC activities. While these processes often function quite well, there are nonetheless opportunities for improvement. In this chapter, we describe USARPAC and I Corps SC planning processes, analyze specific planning issues, and conclude with recommendations.

Overview of the USARPAC and I Corps SC Planning Process

In this chapter, we provide a short overview of planning doctrine as a baseline for comparison with the SC processes used by USARPAC and I Corps and explore why planning for SC might present particular challenges compared to other types of missions.

Doctrine and Security Cooperation Activities Issues

The doctrinal process for planning joint military operations is described in JP 5-0; the Army uses the seven-step military decisionmaking process, which is described in Army Doctrinal Reference Publication 5-0, *The Operations Process*. Both the joint and Army planning processes are informed by design methodology, which provides an approach for understanding the operations environment, defining and framing the problem, and analyzing adversary and friendly strengths and weaknesses. Both of these doctrinal publications also provide guidance on assessment and adjusting the original plan (if necessary).

SC can present special planning challenges. The desired outcomes rarely mesh with the six warfighting functions (mission command, movement and maneuver, intelligence, fires, sustainment, and protection) in an obvious manner.[1] While SC activities are usually conducted as missions, SC is typically performed through key leader engagements, training partner-nation security forces, and conducting combined training with U.S. and partner-nation forces. SC typically occurs during Phase 0 of campaign plans.[2] We were unable to find examples in planning doctrine that specifically addressed operational art and design methodology as applied to SC.[3]

SC-specific guidance only partially addresses these gaps in generic joint and Army planning doctrine. Field Manual 3-22, *Army Support to Security Cooperation*, for example, elaborates on how operational variables can be used to support SC planning, while *Theater Campaign Planning: Planners' Handbook* discusses how to conduct SC planning at both the theater and country levels. Much of existing Army doctrine on operations, including information requirements and orders formats, can in fact be adapted to meet SC guidance needs.[4] Yet even the *Army Security*

---

[1]   See Chapter Three of Army Doctrinal Reference Publication (ADRP) 5-0, *The Operations Process*, Washington, D.C.: Headquarters, Department of the Army, May 17, 2012, for a discussion of the elements of combat power and the six warfighting functions. The principles of joint operations (Objective, Offensive, Mass, Maneuver, Economy of Force, Unity of Command, Security, Surprise, Simplicity, Restraint, Perseverance, and Legitimacy) also provide little doctrinal assistance in designing SC activities. (See Appendix A of JP 5-0, 2011, for a discussion of the principles of joint operations.)

[2]   See JP 5-0, 2011, p. III-39, for a depiction of the notional campaign plan phases.

[3]   Operational art is a U.S. doctrinal concept for planning that links tactical activity to the achievement of strategic goals. Design is "is a methodology for applying critical and creative thinking to understand, visualize, and describe problems and approaches to solving them" (ADRP 5-0, 2012, p. 2-4. Also see U.S. Army Training and Doctrine Command, Training and Doctrine Command Pamphlet 525-5-500, *Commander's Appreciation and Campaign Design*, Fort Monroe, Va., January 28, 2008.)

[4]   FM 3-22, 2013, pp. 3-5 to 3-9; Office of the Deputy Assistant Secretary of Defense for Plans, *Theater Campaign Planning: Planners' Handbook*, Washington, D.C.: Office of the Deputy Assistant Secretary of Defense for Plans, February 2012, pp. 8–25.

Cooperation Handbook acknowledges that "the lack of SC doctrine risks the efficiency and effectiveness of SC activities" and contributes to inconsistent planning, resourcing, and assessment processes across theaters.[5]

One of these gaps in doctrine concerns how Army forces should adapt cross-echelon coordination structures to unique SC demands. In many SC events, low-level executing units need to communicate with high-level planners, with the intervening echelons responsible primarily for unit assignment and administrative support. Standard doctrine assumes that objectives and plans narrow in scope at some or all of the many levels separating a four-star strategic command from a tactical unit operating on the ground. The doctrinal requirement that commander's intent should be clearly understood two echelons down reflects this assumption, but this may not be sufficient for SC activities.[6]

USARPAC has adapted the flow of SC information, including guidance, to encompass multiple echelons at once. For example, large-scale USARPAC SC efforts, such as the Pacific Pathways exercise series, involve each USARPAC echelon down to the brigade level in the planning process, with brigade planners participating alongside USARPAC desk officers and I Corps planners during exercise conferences. However, USARPAC's smaller SC activities often require that a company- or platoon-level element execute an activity that was planned entirely at the four-star USARPAC headquarters level. Furthermore, joint and Army doctrine say little about how a low-level tactical unit should execute an SC activity to best support strategic-level partnership objectives.

The paucity of doctrine regarding tactical unit conduct of SC was reflected in our interviews. According to almost all of our tactical-level interlocutors, planners and executing units rarely refer to SC doctrine while preparing for or carrying out an SC event.[7] One interviewee

---

[5]   Department of the Army Pamphlet 11-31, 2015, p. 6.

[6]   ADRP 5-0, 2012, p. 1-5.

[7]   The material in this chapter draws heavily on a series of interviews we conducted with members of USARPAC and I Corps staffs, April 21–22, 2015, at Fort Shafter, Hawaii; USARPAC staff, November 2–4, 2015, at Fort Shafter; the I Corps liaison officer to USARPAC, I Corps staff, and subordinate headquarters, November 11–13, 2015, at Joint Base Lewis-McChord, Washington; and USARPAC staff, February 10, 2016, at Fort Shafter.

stated that SC-specific doctrine "isn't relevant" to commanders and staff at the brigade or battalion levels, who rely instead on experience, continuity, and warfighting doctrine. Another interviewee suggested that the responsibility for following SC doctrine rested with higher headquarters, stating: "We don't use any SC doctrine . . . anything doctrinally relevant will be in the USARPAC or I Corps order and we will pull it from there."

Given the lack of expertise in SC planning in most staffs below the corps level, as well as gaps in doctrine as it applies to SC at the tactical level, these views are understandable. While manning constraints prevent the Army from assigning dedicated SC planners to brigade and lower-level headquarters staff, the Army could address the doctrinal gap. Improved tactical-level SC doctrine could provide both executing units and planners with a common approach to facing the challenges of coordination, information sufficiency, and guidance regarding objectives, as discussed later in this chapter. Until then, the responsibility to interpret and adapt doctrine to meet the demands of SC rests primarily with higher headquarters, particularly USARPAC and I Corps.[8]

USARPAC SC Planning

According to its mission statement,

> USARPAC postures and prepares the force for unified land operations, responds to threats, sustains and protects the force, and builds military relationships that develop partner defense capacity to contribute to a stable and secure U.S. Pacific Command area of responsibility.[9]

To carry out its mission to build relationships and partner capacity, USARPAC conducts SC planning for unified land operations across

---

[8]   We note that a more robust consideration of SC within the U.S. professional military education system would help to ameliorate many of these shortfalls. However, we do not address this issue here as it is beyond the purview of USARPAC and I Corps—although USARPAC could certainly advocate for such a change within Army professional military education.

[9]   This is the USARPAC mission as stated on its web page (USARPAC, "USARPAC: One Team," website, undated.)

Figure 2.1
U.S. Army Pacific Campaign Process

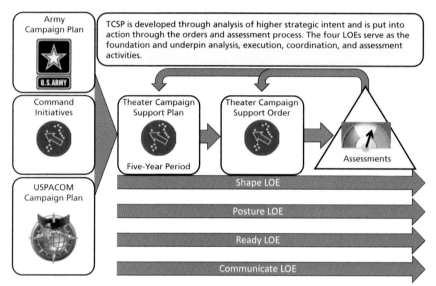

SOURCE: Benjamin A. Bennett, *Integrating Landpower in the Indo–Asia–Pacific Through 2020: Analysis of a Theater Army Campaign Design*, briefing to the Association of the United States Army National Convention, October 14, 2015b; Benjamin A. Bennett, *Integrating Landpower in the Indo–Asia–Pacific Through 2020: Analysis of a Theater Army Campaign Design*, Arlington, Va.: Association of the United States Army, Institute of Land Warfare, The Land Warfare Papers, No. 107, May 2015a, p. 8.
NOTE: LOE = line of effort.
RAND RR1920-2.1

the theater. As depicted in at the top of Figure 2.1, the full campaign process includes assessments, which are discussed in Chapter Three.

USARPAC conducts Army SC planning at multiple levels, ranging from the multiyear Theater Campaign Support Plan (TCSP) through country-specific Engagement Resource Plans (ERPs) and finally down to orders for specific SC activities. USARPAC crafts its TCSP to provide theater-wide guidance for Army efforts in support of USPACOM's Theater Campaign Plan (TCP).[10] The most recent

---

[10] The TCP follows strategic guidance laid out in the Guidance for Employment of the Force, the Joint Strategic Capabilities Plan, and other national-level policy documents;

TCSP lays out nine categories of campaign objectives, including three that focus on SC: "Allies and Partners," "Partner Nation Capacity," and "India." The TCSP additionally describes four LOEs used to accomplish these objectives, with SC activities falling primarily under the "Shape" LOE. USARPAC also drafts its own country-specific ERPs, which combine guidance from the theater-level TCSP and USPACOM's country-level Country Security Cooperation Plans to create a slate of engagement objectives and activities for each USARPAC partner country.[11]

USARPAC holds a number of coordinating events throughout the year to synchronize SC efforts across different scales and echelons, in parallel with the development of formal plans and orders. These events include the Engagement Development Working Group and Security Cooperation Working Group meetings, which provide inputs to USARPAC's country plans as well as subsequent USPACOM-led planning conferences. Security cooperation plans are further refined through contact with host nation counterparts, including in the annual Executive Steering Group meetings that USARPAC holds with select partner nations. Each of these coordinating events brings together staff from USARPAC, I Corps, and sometimes planners from division headquarters.

I Corps SC Planning for Large- and Small-Scale Exercises

As the largest Army operational command assigned to the Pacific theater, I Corps is tasked with carrying out a large portion of USARPAC SC activities. These include the Pacific Pathways series of brigade-level exercises, as well as a wide variety of smaller events.[12]

Figure 2.2 maps the flow of SC guidance between different scales and echelons as it feeds into the planning of these activities.

Office of the Deputy Assistant Secretary of Defense for Plans, 2012, p. 8.

[11] Additionally, USPACOM develops a TSCP that is derived from the Theater Campaign Plan.

[12] Pacific Pathways employs individual units for a series of connected exercises over a period of several months to build upon previous training and make the most efficient use of transportation assets, primarily shipping of unit heavy equipment. For an overview, see USARPAC, "Pacific Pathways 2016: U.S. Army Pacific Readiness and the Strategic Rebalance," pamphlet, undated.

Figure 2.2
Security Cooperation Process Map

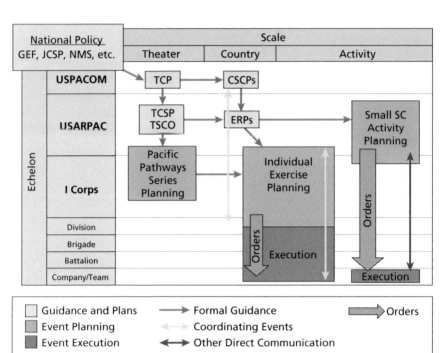

NOTE: CSCP = Country Security Cooperation Plan; GEF = Guidance for the Employment of the Force; JSCP = Joint Strategic Capabilities Plan; NMS = National Military Strategy; TSCO = Theater Support Campaign Order.
RAND RR1920-2.2

Formal guidance for specific SC events is transmitted through orders. While USARPAC provides strategic guidance on Pacific Pathways, including the participating countries and exercise types, I Corps plans and issues the operations orders for the entire yearlong exercise series as well as the individual exercises held with each partner nation. Planning conferences are also held prior to each of the Pacific Pathways exercises, following the Joint Event Life Cycle process.[13] These conferences include participants from USARPAC, I Corps, division, brigade,

---

[13] Chairman of the Joint Chiefs of Staff Manual 3500.O3D, "Joint Training Manual for the Armed Forces of the United States," Washington, D.C.: August 15, 2012, p. E-8.

and sub-brigade echelons. As a large-scale effort that easily divides into smaller components, Pacific Pathways provides I Corps and each of its subordinate echelons the opportunity to exercise mission command.

Planning and issuing guidance for smaller SC activities follows a different process. USARPAC issues the originating orders for these smaller activities, many of which are carried out by small units or ad hoc teams of personnel working at the company level or below. The echelons in between, including I Corps, division, and brigade head-quarters, are responsible for assigning forces, deconflicting with other tasks, and passing USARPAC guidance down the orders chain. Once this formal echelon-by-echelon process is complete, executing units and USARPAC planners tend to communicate directly by phone or email, speeding up coordination in preparation for the SC event.

Specific Planning Issues

The sections that follow consider how SC planning works in practice for USARPAC and I Corps and the issues that affect that process.

Coordination Processes Work Adequately, But Several Problems Remain

Planning and executing an SC event requires extensive coordination on the part of USARPAC, I Corps, and executing units. The existing coordination system is built on the formal orders chain, multiechelon planning conferences, and other direct communications, as described above. This system generally functions well, though challenges remain.

Several coordination problems identified by interviewees were caused by inconsistent adherence to established practice rather than problems with the system itself. Some of these departures from standard practice appear rooted in growing pains associated with recent changes to the relationship between USARPAC and I Corps. These changes include USARPAC becoming a four-star command, the formal assign-ment of I Corps to USARPAC, the transfer of 25th Infantry Divi-sion (25ID) from USARPAC to I Corps' command, and the transfer of primary planning responsibility for Pacific Pathways exercises from

USARPAC to I Corps. The last two changes in particular have required adjustment in USARPAC and I Corps' coordination processes. USAR-PAC and I Corps are aware of and have addressed some of these issues already. One I Corps interviewee stated that there recently have been noticeable improvements in guidance from USARPAC to I Corps.[14]

Interviews and other documents often stressed the importance of the formal echelon-to-echelon orders process. Informal, direct communication is good for some purposes, while orders are important for others. Formal orders serve as an explicit record of objectives, tasks, and responsibilities and thus provide accountability and a common point of reference for an event across echelons and staff sections. The formal orders chain also provides I Corps and its subordinate echelons the opportunity to assign forces and ensure that SC tasks do not conflict with other activities that a higher echelon might be unaware of. Finally, adherence to the formal orders process strengthens the multiechelon mission command system, which was one of the reasons for unifying large exercises under Pacific Pathways and placing them under I Corps.

USARPAC has at times directly tasked 25ID with carrying out SC activities, rather than following standard procedure and routing orders through I Corps. As one interviewee stated, this can cause problems because 25ID may have other requirements of which USARPAC is unaware. This is reportedly now less of a problem than it was in previous years. While USARPAC orders still sometimes designate 25ID as the executing unit, particularly for events with the division's habitual partner units, these orders are generally routed through I Corps.[15] USARPAC and 25ID remain in close contact for SC planning; this is unsurprising, given their collocation in Hawaii and prior command relationship. As coordination with I Corps improves, the close rela-

---

[14]   On the assignment of I Corps to USARPAC, see Vincent K. Brooks, "U.S. Army Pacific and the Pacific Rebalance," *Army*, October 2013, p. 124.

[15]   Although difficult to measure, it appears that coordination through channels has improved since the beginning of this project. Virtually all of the specific examples reported to us were more than a year old at the time of writing and either preceded or coincided with the realignment USARPAC and I Corps and the transition of Pacific Pathways planning responsibility to I Corps.

tionship between USARPAC and 25ID will remain beneficial without creating coordination difficulties.

Some interviewees described the current division of responsibilities for Pacific Pathways between USARPAC and I Corps as "muddled" or confused. One point of stress for the I Corps–USARPAC relationship is the annual Pacific Pathways order, I Corps' highest-level SC planning responsibility. I Corps drafts and issues this order but relies on USARPAC to provide the strategic guidance. However, some interlocutors perceived that USARPAC does not always provide sufficient strategic guidance and sometimes seeks to return to its prior role of directly managing exercises. Unless strategic goals are clearly established, the risk increases that SC activities will not support the achievement of those goals. For example, if the intent of an engagement is to improve the ability of a partner nation to maintain its own helicopters, but a detachment of U.S. mechanics does not understand that this is the objective, the U.S. soldiers might spend all of their efforts repairing host-nation helicopters.

Most interviewees agreed that the coordinating conferences for the Pacific Pathways exercise series provide a useful forum for timely communication across echelons. These conferences were not seen as a substitute for formal orders, however, and participants did not always come away with a clear understanding of activity objectives, plans, and responsibilities. Interviewees at the brigade and battalion levels stated that in some instances, information from the conferences was not adequately captured and transmitted to the executing unit planners. Interviewees reported a case in which during planning, the partner nation expressed the intent to invite U.S. officers to an officer's club event that would require coat and tie. This was not communicated to the participating unit, which brought shorts and sandals for civilian clothing.

It appears that planning conference outcomes were not captured in any single, authoritative record. Additionally, some interviewees stated that different meeting participants frequently came away with differing impressions of exercise goals. They also noted that many important people do not attend these meetings. For instance, although a battalion planner might attend the conference, that planner is seldom the same one who will be with the battalion when it actually executes the events. Consequently, the people executing the event must rely on accurately capturing and disseminating the planning details provided at the conference.[16]

These planning events did, however, often provide participants enough information to begin planning for an event and sometimes also served as venues for executing units to connect with their partner-nation counterparts. Holding conferences earlier in the event planning cycle might provide an opportunity for bottom-up refinement of plans, which some interviewees mentioned as currently missing from the planning process.

Interviewees also agreed on the importance of low-level executing units' direct contact with USARPAC planners when preparing for SC engagements at the company level and below. However, low-level direct contact is not a substitute for the initial echelon-to-echelon process of assigning units and issuing orders, and such contact properly begins after this process is completed. In fact, I Corps commonly uses the orders chain to formally provide the executing unit with direct liaison authority to the relevant USARPAC point of contact, usually a desk officer. Once units are assigned, direct communication between those involved in an event is a far more efficient way of communicating routine information requirements and changes of plan than going through the formal request for information or orders process. However, direct communication does not appear to always serve as an effective substitute for formal planning and mission command processes. Satisfaction with existing processes appears uneven; some interviewees were satisfied with informal coordination processes, while others were not.[17]

Significant changes, such as those affecting event dates or personnel requirements, might still go through a planning conference memorandum, fragmentary order (FRAGO), or other form of official communication to ensure that intervening echelons are aware of changes that affect their force assignment decisions or other responsibilities.

---

[16] During interviews, perceptions varied on whether it would be desirable to have the same people participate in all of the planning events. However, interviewees agreed that the information gathered had to be passed on to all of the people who require it, yet this often did not occur.

[17] In general, the lower the echelon, the more likely it was that interlocutors expressed dissatisfaction with the timeliness of communications.

Even routine communications should include representatives of intervening echelons when possible. One interviewee stated that his unit frequently coordinated with USARPAC directly over email, but kept I Corps on the "cc" line as a matter of course.

Issuing of Orders Met the Standard, but Lower-Echelon Units Need More Time

An efficient and inclusive coordination system can ease the flow of information between SC planners and executing units. Whether this system provides timely and sufficient information for SC planning is a separate issue.

For the most part, orders were issued by USARPAC in a timely manner in terms of advance notice prior to the event. The exceptions appeared to be cases in which a short-notice event was driven by requirements external to USARPAC, such as a quick turnaround request from a partner nation passed through a country team. Interview respondents also acknowledged that broad orders covering multiple, large events could be issued up to a year ahead of time, which would allow tactical-level units to begin planning for events, even if many of the specifics of the events would be filled in over the course of the year.

Figure 2.3 depicts our calculation of the lead time provided by USARPAC SC orders to I Corps in FY 2015. The majority of USARPAC orders to I Corps were received at least 45 days prior to the start of the SC activity. This generally provided I Corps with enough time— three days if no major changes were needed—to fulfill its own guidance drafting process and send its own order down to the next echelon at least 42 days prior to the event. I Corps formalized these minimum lead times in a 2013 memo on the orders process.

I Corps aims to complete the military decisionmaking process and issue an order to a subordinate unit within 72 hours after receiving an order from USARPAC.[18] We did not have a significant number of orders from both USARPAC and I Corps for the same SC events to judge regarding how often this goal was achieved.

---

[18] "I Corps Orders Writing, Staffing and Publishing," I Corps G3 Memorandum, January 22, 2013.

Figure 2.3
Orders Analysis: Timeliness of SC Orders from USARPAC to I Corps

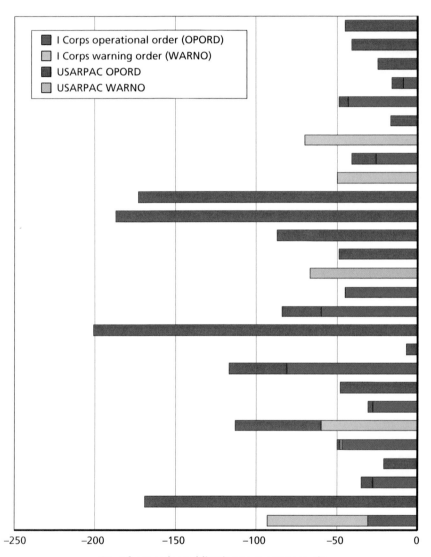

Days from order publication to event execution

Although USARPAC and I Corps may have in most cases met a standard of issuing orders to executing units at least 42 days in advance, planners at the division and brigade levels reported that they expected much longer lead times, as indicated by the "1/3–2/3 rule." The "1/3– 2/3 rule" suggests that higher headquarters consume no more than one-third of the time available for planning, allowing subordinate commands the remaining two-thirds of the time to conduct the more in-depth planning necessary at lower levels. Despite this expectation among tactical-level leaders and planners, a majority of those we interviewed reported that the "1/3–2/3 rule" is rarely followed.

Some interviewees at USARPAC and I Corps headquarters posited that the "1/3–2/3 rule"[19] does not apply to SC activities. It is unclear in planning doctrine whether SC events should follow training versus operational timelines. This may result from a lack of doctrinal examples of how operational art is applied to SC. Nonetheless, there was a clear expectation among many brigade- and lower-level planners that higher headquarters should follow the "1/3–2/3 rule." Perceptions varied widely regarding the impact when OPORDs were late. A majority of interview-ees stated that attendance at the planning conferences effectively pro-vided a WARNO with sufficient information to begin parallel planning. Others disagreed—but provided only a handful of examples in which their own planning and execution was affected due to lack of a timely OPORD. These were primarily related to partner-nation customs and equipment shipping issues (e.g., different partner nations have different requirements for DD-1750 formatting).

Planners at all echelons told us there are several workarounds to the "1/3–2/3 rule," enabling an executing unit to begin planning for an

---

[19] According to Army planning doctrine:

> When allocating planning time to staffs, commanders must ensure subordinates have enough time to plan and prepare their own actions prior to execution. Commanders follow the "one-third–two-thirds rule" as a guide to allocate time available. They use one-third of the time available before execution for their planning and allocate the remaining two-thirds of the time available before execution to their subordinates for planning and preparation (ADRP 5-0, 2012, p. 2-23).

We are aware of no written arguments that SC planning is an exception to this particular rule of thumb.

SC event before receiving an OPORD or a FRAGO. While keeping in mind the importance of a formal orders process as discussed above, examples of such workarounds include WARNOs, heads-up emails, brigade and division planner participation in USARPAC exercise planning conferences, and sharing drafts of orders across multiple echelons. Additionally, multiple echelons participate in I Corps operations planning teams. This practice supports parallel planning and provides a forum to identify information that is required but has not yet been provided. Through participation in the I Corps' operations planning teams, division- and brigade-level planners get the USARPAC order at virtually the same time as the corps, providing the maximum amount of time to request additional information if necessary.

Nonetheless, workarounds and opportunities for parallel planning do not remove the need for efficiency in the formal orders process. Interviewees mentioned that units that received late guidance might lack sufficient time to conduct mission analysis or face difficulties in meeting passport and other travel requirements on short notice. For example, according to multiple interviewees, the State Department requires flight schedules and passenger manifests before issuing official passports. However, the turnaround time for issuing passports takes so long that this information is usually not available to the units by the deadline for submitting passport applications.[20] In its report on regionally aligned forces, the GAO found that USAFRICOM also faced these travel problems.[21]

---

[20] We did not independently confirm passport guidance or processing times. Several interviewees reported that the State Department guidelines requires applications six months before the passports are needed and requires travel tickets to have been issued with an itinerary provided before processing passport requests; however, DoD will not arrange itineraries and cut tickets less than 30 days prior to travel.

[21] GAO, "Regionally Aligned Forces: DoD Could Enhance Army Brigades' Efforts in Africa by Improving Activity Coordination and Mission-Specific Preparation," GAO-15-568, August 2015, pp. 35–39.

Planning Information Tended to Lack Specific Information for SC Events

We reviewed several dozen USARPAC and I Corps orders to determine whether they contained the basic information needed to conduct SC events.[22] We found that the standard information typically found in orders for warfighting or stability operations missions was routinely present. However, information related specifically to SC events—links to USPACOM or USARPAC strategic objectives, results of earlier SC

Figure 2.4
Presence of Basic Information in Orders

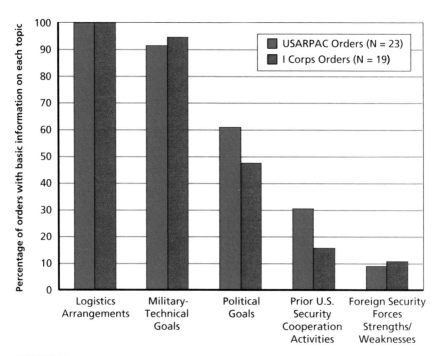

---

[22] This set of orders included all USARPAC security cooperation orders to I Corps in FY 2015, and a partial set of I Corps security cooperation orders to its subordinates in FY 2015. For information on the sources of these orders, see the methods section at the beginning of this chapter. Our coding scheme is described in Appendix A.

events, and the capabilities of participating partner-nation units—were not frequently present. Figure 2.4 depicts a summary of this analysis.

The results of our interviews with planners at below-corps levels were consistent with our analysis of USARPAC and I Corps orders. The vast majority of interviewees reported that their focus was on their own unit's readiness; SC was a means to improve/sustain readiness but not viewed as an end itself at their level. There appeared to be no specific template or checklist for SC activities other than the standard "five-paragraph order." Mission types were reported to vary widely—from large exercises involving an entire brigade to subject-matter expert (SME) exchanges involving only a handful of soldiers—making it difficult to establish a boilerplate for concepts of operation.

We most commonly heard that sufficient higher headquarters information was lacking in terms of logistics details, especially regarding unit movement and equipment shipping. Lack of accurate guidance regarding differences in partner-nation customs/import requirements was a related issue. A handful of interviewees stated they had to repeatedly redo forms because of conflicting guidance on partner-nation requirements.[56]

Guidance on SC Objectives Lacked Information on Strategic Considerations

In their orders to subordinate units, USARPAC and I Corps do fairly well at communicating logistics arrangements and military-technical goals associated with SC activities, as depicted in Figure 2.4. They are less consistent, however, in providing information on strategic goals. As one interviewee stated, "I have a better sense of what [my partner-nation counterparts] want out of this exercise than what our higher headquarters wants out of it."[23]

---

[23] However, we note that a division transportation officer stated the problem was a training issue with battalion-level planners, not a problem with doctrine or lack of higher-level guidance. According to this officer, the information is readily available, but some battalion-level planners do not know how to find it and apparently do not know they can ask their division transportation officer for this information. (Arroyo Center researcher interviews with I Corps staff and subordinate headquarters, November 11–13, 2015, Joint Base Lewis-McChord.)

Even when information is provided, the connection between strategic goals and tactical-level tasks is rarely specified. A number of interviewees highlighted this problem. As discussed earlier, SC activities pose a unique challenge in that small tactical-level engagements are intended to have effects, at least in the aggregate, on the strategic-level relationship between the U.S. and partner-nation militaries. I Corps and especially USARPAC face the difficult but crucial task of making clear to their subordinates how tactical-level SC tasks can best support their intended strategic-level effects.

Just showing up to an engagement may fulfill some SC objectives, such as demonstrating commitment to the partner nation, making U.S. access to partner-nation military personnel and facilities more routine, or maintaining a U.S. Army presence in theater in case of unexpected contingencies. However, most other SC objectives, such as building partner capacity or developing close relationships with foreign security forces, depend more on the focused efforts of the executing unit. A unit is more likely to be effective at SCC if it knows which of these objectives it should support, how to prioritize them, and how specific tasks connect to these objectives.

Providing lengthy reference documents containing SC guidance does little to address this gap. These documents are vague (at least when one is searching for event-specific guidance) and can easily overwhelm an executing unit with their sheer volume. As one interviewee stated, strategy guidance can consume hundreds of pages without saying anything useful at the tactical level. Guidance on event objectives needs to be clear, relevant, and concise if it is to be read and applied by an executing unit. Fortunately, two frameworks are already in widespread use that can help communicate this guidance: the doctrinal five-paragraph orders format and USARPAC's country-level ERPs.

According to ADRP 5-0,

> The commander's intent is a clear and concise expression of the purpose of the operation and the desired military end state that supports mission command, provides focus to the staff, and helps subordinate and supporting commanders act to achieve the com-

mander's desired results without further orders, even when the operation does not unfold as planned.[24]

Yet our review of USARPAC and I Corps SC orders found that this guidance was often vague, redundant, or disconnected from specified tasks. One USARPAC order, for instance, directed I Corps to provide a small team to help a partner nation improve its aviation maintenance program. The commander's intent specified three end states: (1) a strengthened bilateral relationship, (2) increased maintenance capability within the partner aviation unit, and (3) improved partner-nation self-defense capability. The first and third end goals are too vague and high-level to relate to a maintenance team's daily activities; the second end goal is too obvious to offer additional information on carrying out the team's task.

It is possible to craft guidance that avoids the trap of being too vague or too obvious, although it requires careful thought about the dilemmas faced at the tactical level and the potential tradeoffs between different goals. To take the above example, a helicopter maintenance team might have to choose between several potentially conflicting objectives. These might include the following:

- Should capacity building efforts focus on short-term or long-term capacity building needs? Long-term partner capacity building efforts might focus on maintenance fundamentals, tracking and anticipating maintenance needs, or helping partners design a curriculum to train future maintainers. In contrast, short-term training might be designed to alleviate the unit's most immediate maintenance needs or keep as many aircraft available for pilot training as possible.[25]
- How should the unit balance partner-nation goals with U.S. priorities? The broad parameters for this balance will have been determined by U.S. country team personnel in coordination with partner-nation officials and USARPAC. But the same need to bal-

---

[24] ADRP 5-0, 2012, p. 1–5.

[25] We also note that that the training received by partner-nation forces perishes over a certain period of time. One-off events are less likely to be sustained.

ance a partner's needs with U.S. objectives also appears at tactical levels, and different tactical planners may reach different conclusions about how to strike this balance—especially in the absence of clear guidance.

- How important is interoperability? The maintenance team should be provided guidance on whether to focus on teaching U.S.-specific systems and practices to improve interoperability or to adapt their skills to improve the partner's own systems and practices, even if these are not easily compatible with standard U.S. approaches.
- How much effort should go into relationship building? The team should be provided guidance on whether to focus as much as possible on building partner capacity versus prioritizing social time with their partner-nation counterparts to build rapport and make a good impression, even if this means reducing time spent on technical military objectives.
- How much effort should the maintenance team spend on maintaining its own readiness, as opposed to building partner capacity? If the team's usual readiness requirements include training others or confronting the same maintenance challenges, these goals may substantially overlap, but this is not always the case. Striking the right balance between these two goals is particularly relevant when units accustomed to focusing on their own capability development are asked to conduct SC engagements.
- Are there any secondary objectives? For example, the unit could be told that the maintenance training is tied to other U.S. priorities, such as supporting U.S. foreign military sales (FMS).

Good strategic guidance would help the team prioritize in the face of the above types of tactical-level dilemmas.

In this specific case, some (but not all) of this guidance existed, but it was scattered across different documents. The USARPAC order to I Corps included the goal of keeping as many partner-nation aircraft at full operational capability as possible to support the unit's training, but this was left out of the I Corps order to the executing unit. Both the USARPAC and I Corps orders mentioned the goal of improving the partner unit's organic maintenance training capability. And on a classified network, unreferenced by either order, the Engagement Resource Plan discussed the importance of aviation maintenance in supporting FMS and interoperability with this partner nation. Neither FMS nor interoperability were mentioned in either the USARPAC or I Corps order, even though these objectives clearly apply to this engagement.

Orders guidance, no matter how thoughtful, does not always make it all the way from the engagement planners to the executing unit intact. Each echelon, as part of mission command, reformats and revises an order before sending it down the chain, providing multiple opportunities for a key objective to be lost in transmission. If possible, the cross-echelon process should be turned into a quality-assuring, rather than quality-reducing, step in the process.

Providing each echelon easy cross-echelon access to concise, relevant guidance associated with particular countries and common event types in theater can help it double-check guidance in orders from higher headquarters and clarify whether it is missing any potentially important objectives.

Relevant, event-specific guidance that survives the orders process intact should be sufficient on its own to carry out an SC activity. But to provide additional context and redundancy, concise guidance associated with the partner country could also be provided with little extra effort. Much of this guidance is already found in existing ERPs, which discuss SC priorities for each of USARPAC's partner nations.[26] The ERPs are updated annually, which should be sufficiently frequent, given the long-term nature of most bilateral SC objectives. The ERPs are also quite concise—generally only two to five pages. While they are currently stored on SIPRNET, most of their SC-related content is unclassified, so a cleaned-up version could be transferred to NIPRNET. Once there, it would be much easier to attach these clean versions to SC orders, which are generally transmitted over NIPRNET. It would also be easier to

---

[26] One interviewee even described the ERP as the single-most important USARPAC product for communicating SC guidance. Researcher notes from meeting with I Corps staff, April 2015.

maintain unclassified ERPs on a shared portal site, organized by country and accessible across USARPAC, I Corps, and subordinate echelons.

Global Theater Security Cooperation Management Information System (G-TSCMIS) has the potential to be a repository of such information, but at the time of writing we found that it was not routinely used by USARPAC and its subordinate units. Rather, USARPAC used Strategic Management System (SMS) as its SC system of record, not G-TSCMIS.[27]

In some cases, other relevant guidance documents may be worth attaching to an order. If the event was motivated by a particular senior leader engagement, an executive summary or notes from those meetings could also be included. Of course, many senior leader engagements cover sensitive topics that may not be suitable for widespread distribution. In these cases, a "sanitized" record of the engagement might be distributed instead. When sensitive information is relevant to SC (such as a partner-nation military officer providing a surprisingly critical assessment of his or her unit's capabilities), it can often be cleaned up or toned down to still provide useful context for an executing unit.

At times, USARPAC or I Corps can usefully provide guidance on a particular type of SC event. If a particular SC engagement is part of a larger series of engagements carried out across the theater, guidance specific to that event type, rather than the partner country, might be included. In the case of Pacific Pathways or logistics SME exchanges, concise guidance already exists in the form of theater-wide engagement orders. Such guidance could be developed further for other common types of SC engagements, such as disaster response and resilience exchanges or aviation maintenance support teams.

---

[27] The use of G-TSCMIS is mandated by several policies. However, a Center for Army Lessons Learned bulletin on security cooperation noted that "It currently acts mainly as a system to record events more than as a tool to plan and synchronize future events. Numerous ASCCs [Army service component commands] report being challenged to stay abreast of engagements by subordinate units" (Center for Army Lessons Learned, "Bulletin 16-09: Security Cooperation: Lessons and Best Practices," March 2016). A full assessment of G-TSCMIS per se is beyond the scope of this study and the topic of ongoing RAND work led by Jeff Marquis and David Thaler. Nonetheless, at the time of writing it appeared that G-TSCMIS did not have the full range of capabilities needed to capture all of the information needed for SC planning at the ASCC and corps levels.

It should not be necessary for executing units to refer to higher-level documents, such as USARPAC's TCSP or USPACOM's TCP and Country Security Cooperation Plans. All portions of those documents relevant to Army SC at the country level should already be incorporated into the ERPs for each partner nation. In general, guidance should follow two mutually supporting principles: It should be relevant and concise so that it is actually read. This applies to both formal orders and any reference documents.

USARPAC theater-level plans are lengthy, thorough, and complex, as befits the product of a robust planning process. They are not, however, easily referenced by a tactical-level unit concerned with carrying out a specific type of SC event with a specific partner. The same applies even more to USPACOM, Army service, and national-level planning documents. Part of USARPAC's job is to relieve lower echelons of the need to sift through these plans (and their annexes, and the appendices to their annexes) to find the information relevant to executing a particular SC activity.

Shortages Exist in People and Funding

Virtually every headquarters said they were understaffed for all functions, not just SC, because they were well below 100 percent of required strength. We note, however, that this is not a challenge unique to SC activities. Several planners said that planning for non-SC events, such as combat training center rotations, were an additional source of stress upon staffs.[28] Interviewees from one battalion stated they could handle planning for a combat training center rotation or a Pacific Pathways deployment, but doing both at the same time—with one event directly following another—stretched the staff to the limit.

Interviewees at I Corps reported they believe that a newly funded General Schedule position for SC planning will be useful, but the person had not yet been hired at the time of writing. Interviewees at

---

[28] We also note that combat training center rotations, as well as many other non-SC tasks, are driven by requirements from U.S. Army Forces Command. In a sense, I Corps serves two four-star masters. One of its responsibilities is to deconflict requirements issued by USARPAC and U.S. Army Forces Command.

the 7th Infantry Division stated that additional people for SC planning would be helpful only if they were full time. The brigade and below consensus was that part-time help does not add value because of the requirement to get them up to speed. (However, increasing headquarters staffing would always be welcome.)

Several interviewees stated that the timeliness of letters of authorization (LOAs) is problematic. Others mentioned "color of money" issues. However, it appears this may be more of a coordination and training problem than lack of funding per se. The statutes and authorities regarding what funds can be spent on which SC activities are complex and often inadequately understood at the lower echelons. According to Department of Army SC officials, this is a common challenge across all of the theater armies.[29]

Coordinating Between the Shape and Ready LOEs

As discussed earlier, interviewees at echelons below corps level consistently reported that their sole focus during SC events was to improve the readiness of their own unit. While they also stated that they generally recognized the importance of cultural understanding, training partner-nation units or staffs, and cordially cooperating with partner-nation units and personnel, the only outcomes they considered as specific objectives to be attained were directly linked to readiness outcomes, such as mission essential task proficiency. These interviews suggest that tensions exist between the goals and execution of the Shape and Ready lines of effort (LOEs) of the USARPAC TCSP. Subsequent discussions with general officer–level interlocutors indicated that these tensions have generally gone unresolved.

Doctrine does not provide specific guidance regarding the coordination or synchronization of LOEs. JP 5-0, *Joint Operation Planning*, discusses "nesting" or vertical integration of end states, objectives, effects, and tasks between echelons. The plans and activities of each

---

[29]   Arroyo researcher interviews with Security Cooperation Division, Directorate Strategy, Plans and Policy, personnel, Washington, D.C., January 13, 2016. SC funding is a complex topic that is beyond the scope of this study. However, since USARPAC senior officers asked us to include this subject in our interview questions, we provide this brief summary.

Figure 2.5
Vertical Integration of End States, Objectives, Effects, and Tasks

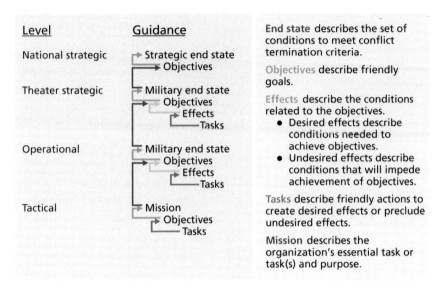

Level	Guidance	
National strategic	Strategic end state, Objectives	End state describes the set of conditions to meet conflict termination criteria.
Theater strategic	Military end state, Objectives, Effects, Tasks	Objectives describe friendly goals. Effects describe the conditions related to the objectives.
Operational	Military end state, Objectives, Effects, Tasks	• Desired effects describe conditions needed to achieve objectives. • Undesired effects describe conditions that will impede achievement of objectives.
Tactical	Mission, Objectives, Tasks	Tasks describe friendly actions to create desired effects or preclude undesired effects. Mission describes the organization's essential task or task(s) and purpose.

SOURCE: JP 5-0, 2011, p. III-21.
RAND *RR1920-2.5*

unit should be integrated with those of its higher headquarters, as illustrated in Figure 2.5.

However, JP 5-0 provides little in regard to coordinating or synchronizing activities between the LOEs of any particular echelon. At best, it describes the potential for combining lines of operation (LOOs) and LOEs: "Commanders may use both LOOs and lines of effort to connect objectives to a central, unifying purpose . . . Combining LOOs and lines of effort allows commanders to include nonmilitary activities in their operational design."[30] Yet, how action *y* in one LOE might relate to action *x* in a different LOE is not discussed. One might argue that such coordination or synchronization is either implied by or inherent to operational art and operational design, but this aspect

---

[30] JP 5-0, 2011, p. III-28. LOEs are defined as: "In the context of joint operations planning, using the purpose (cause and effect) to focus efforts toward establishing operational and strategic conditions by linking multiple tasks and missions" (p. GL-12).

of planning and execution is not explicitly addressed within JP 5-0 or ADRP 5-0, *The Operations Process.*[31]

Coordination between activities in different LOEs is particularly challenging between the Ready LOE and the Shape LOE within the USARPAC construct for supporting the USPACOM TCP. The other two LOEs are Posture and Communicate. However, our analysis of interviews at echelons below corps indicated that disconnects between Ready and Shape have the greatest potential to cause "mission fratricide" at the tactical level. This could occur if a unit commander decided that maximizing the readiness of his or her own unit during a combined training event required sacrificing the building of partner capacity or maintaining military-to-military relationships.

The TCSP describes the Ready LOE as "what we do to ourselves," while the Shape LOE entails "actions we take to impact something other than us." The Ready LOE, which involves increasing or sustaining the readiness of units assigned or attached to USARPAC, may be challenging or complicated, but it involves processes and procedures that are well-known and well-defined at each echelon. Unit readiness is routinely measured using the Chairman of the Joint Chiefs of Staff Readiness System.[32]

Shape, however, is a complex, ill-structured, or "wicked" problem.[33] Whereas U.S. commanders can direct the actions of U.S. units to achieve Ready goals, Shape goals can only be achieved indirectly, by influencing the actions of partners. Moreover, progress in executing the tasks and achieving the intermediate objectives along each LOE moves at a different pace. Unit readiness tasks are executed on a peri-

---

[31] ADRP 5-0, 2012.

[32] Chairman of the Joint Chiefs of Staff, *CJCS Guide to the Chairman's Readiness System*, Office of the Chairman of the Joint Chiefs of Staff, CJCS Guide 3401D, November 15, 2010, pp. 7–20. JP 1-02 defines "readiness," as "the ability of United States military forces to fight and meet the demands of the national military strategy." It is composed of "unit readiness" or the ability of units to execute their assigned missions and the ability of combatant commanders "to integrate and synchronize ready combat and support forces to execute his or her assigned missions" (JP 1-02, 2016, p. 198).

[33] For a discussion of operational problem types, see Training and Doctrine Command Pamphlet 525-5-500, 2008, pp. 8–12.

odic routine. For example, tank or Stryker gunnery is usually conducted semiannually. The average brigade combat team experiences a combat training center rotation roughly every other year. Conversely, it can take years, if not decades, to alter defense relationships with partner nations, and the milestones along the way can be ambiguous. Although it is common to refer to synchronization of effects, these two LOEs have such different characteristics that coordination is likely to be a more plausible goal.[34]

The USARPAC approach to this challenge is to assign a senior officer (often a general officer) as champion for each LOE and make him or her responsible for developing processes and procedures to synchronize activities between his or her LOE and the other LOEs. The champion for each LOE is also supported by a staff section that is designated to be the office of primary responsibility for that LOE. The LOE champions use the Executive Steering Board (ESB) as a primary mechanism to coordinate activities amongst LOEs.

The ESB meets quarterly and consists of the USARPAC commanding general and deputy commanders supported by key staff. According to the former chief of Strategy and Policy within USARPAC G-5:

> USARPAC implemented a two-part Campaign Assessment Process with the intent of recognizing whether environmental conditions were receptive to campaign inputs, whether those inputs were achieving the intended consequence and how the resulting changes would influence future activities. This process includes specific Environmental and Campaign Assessments that are integrated during the Executive Steering Board to provide increased overall awareness . . . This board provides the commander the opportunity to assess the environment, understand the status

---

[34] ADP 3-0 defines synchronization as "Synchronization is the arrangement of military actions in time, space, and purpose to produce maximum relative combat power at a decisive place and time (JP 2-0). It is the ability to execute multiple related and mutually supporting tasks in different locations at the same time, producing greater effects than executing each in isolation" (p. 2-4).

of key initiatives, identify opportunities and potential setbacks, receive staff inputs and decide on campaign adjustments.[35]

USARPAC personnel indicated that the ESB not only performs assessments of the theater environment and progress in executing the theater campaign plan but often results in commander's guidance.

Our limited analysis of this process suggests that the ESB is a useful forum for coordination between LOEs.[36] However, the results of such coordination between USARPAC Ready and Shape LOEs was not obvious when discussing tactical execution with personnel from units at echelons below corps: The focus was almost entirely on readiness with little awareness of shaping objectives. In our planning recommendations below, we suggest that SC strategic objectives be communicated to all echelons in either the commander's intent or concept of operations paragraphs within the relevant orders. If this recommendation is implemented by USARPAC, the champions (or offices of primary responsibility) for the Ready and Shape LOEs may wish to conduct oversight to confirm that orders include guidance on linking activities between the LOEs. In other words, if Ready LOE activity x is intended to support Shape LOE objective y, they might verify that orders received by the executing tactical unit contain that information.

This chapter has provided an overview of the planning process for SC events at USARPAC and I Corps. It has also identified a number of issues with that process, including the coordination of SC events, the timeliness of the orders issued for those events, and the adequacy of the information provided with those orders. Additionally, it identified the larger issues of staffing and funding and the inherent tension between unit readiness and participation in SC activities and unit readiness. In the next chapter, we address evaluation of USARPAC and I Corps SC events.

---

[35]   Bennett, 2015a, pp. 8–9.

[36]   Our analysis was limited in this aspect as we were initially asked to focus on processes and interactions between USARPAC and I Corps and the echelons below corps. For most of this study we treated USARPAC as a "black box" that produced direction and provided resources, but the internal processes of USARPAC were beyond scope.

CHAPTER THREE

USARPAC Strategic and Tactical Evaluation of SC Activities

Introduction

Evaluation is a key component of every step of the SC decision cycle. As Figure 3.1 depicts, planning and evaluation are mutually reinforcing. Planners identify what needs to be done based on an evaluation of prior interactions with partner countries and U.S. objectives, how it will be done, and what resources will be required to do it. Evaluators assess outputs and outcomes from SC activities based on objectives specified by planners and feed the results of their assessment back to the planners.

We evaluated SC evaluation processes at both the strategic and tactical levels in this AOR through interviews with personnel at USARPAC and I Corps, analyses of AARs from SC events, and analyses of existing USARPAC evaluation tools. We supplemented these analyses with a review of secondary literature, including U.S. military doctrine,

Figure 3.1
Recursive Planning and Evaluation Cycle

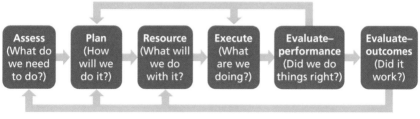

RAND *RR1920-3.1*

official guidance, and the broader literature on best practices for monitoring and evaluation.

Our analysis of USARPAC's evaluation procedures found that although many of the components necessary for integrating evaluation into each step of the SC decision cycle are in place, critical information is missing. USARPAC's evaluation process breaks down in two places. First, at a conceptual level, USARPAC's strategic evaluation process often does a poor job specifying the causal relationships between tactical activities and strategic objectives. Second, much of the data that would be necessary to make informed evaluations are not currently collected. We believe that tactical-level units could help fill this gap.[1] A combination of better data collection and management could increase the quality and quantity of information available to operational and strategic planners. Many SC activities are conducted with committed partners and are definitely strategically important, but it still may be difficult to link this strategic importance to actual tactical activities. For such activities, rigorous impact evaluations can test whether the desired outputs or outcomes are being achieved. This chapter examines USARPAC's evaluation process at the strategic and tactical levels.

Strategic Evaluation

Strategic evaluation enables USARPAC to evaluate whether its SC activities have helped accomplish its strategic objectives; update its set of SC activities in light of lessons learned and progress toward strategic objectives; and provide feedback and guidance to tactical units to execute their SC-related missions. USARPAC's strategic evaluation process is based on three main components:

1. professional judgment from senior officers responsible for evaluating each of USARPAC's LOEs (LOE managers)

---

[1]   Another option could be the use of strategic debriefers in units such as the 500th Military Intelligence Brigade.

2. country environmental assessments (Political, Military, Economic, Social, Infrastructure, and Information [PMESII] framework)
3. assessments of how SC activities contribute to strategic objectives (SMS framework).

Of these three, the role of the LOE manager is predominant. In contrast, the SMS framework is often ignored due to concerns over quality of information. We believe that strengthening USARPAC's strategic evaluation process depends on improving the usefulness of the SMS framework.

Procedures for Execution and Evaluation at Strategic and Tactical Levels Have Some Limitations

As defined by Joint Publication 3-0, *Joint Operations*, assessment is the "determination of the progress toward accomplishing a task, creating a condition, or achieving an objective."[2] Army-specific guidance for implementing a continuous assessment process cycle is detailed in Army Doctrinal Reference Publication 5-0, The Operations Process, which discusses monitoring, evaluating, and recommending action for improvement.[3] Tools typically used for assessing the progress of an operation include the Operations Order, Common Operating Picture, personal observations, the use of running estimates and the assessment plan.[4]

All echelons have roles to play in the evaluation process, with each echelon employing metrics appropriate to its level of activity. Figure 3.2 lays out the assessment activities specific to tactical, operational, theater strategic, and national strategic levels.[5] Planning for assessment begins upon receipt of the mission from higher headquarters, when planners need to assess objectives, end states, and how to accomplish given tasks. They must ensure that the objectives, effects, and activities are mea-

---

[2]   JP 3-0, *Joint Operations*, Washington, D.C.: Chairman of the Joint Chiefs of Staff, August 11, 2011.

[3]   ADRP 5-0, 2012.

[4]   FM 6-0, *Commander and Staff Organization and Operations*, Washington, D.C.: Headquarters, Department of the Army, Field Manual, May 2014, p. 15-2.

[5]   JP 5-0, 2011.

Figure 3.2
Army Assessment Levels and Measures

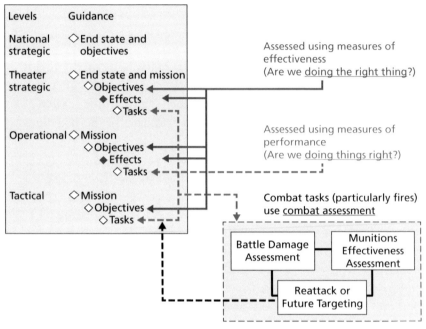

SOURCE: JP 5-0, Figure D-1, p. D-7.i.
RAND RR1920-3.2

sureable as a means of evaluating activities and build upon current guidance from the TCSP, TSCO, and base OPORD. As part of the planning process, strategic planners identify appropriate measures of performance and effectiveness for tactical and operational levels. This process enables planners to envision what success looks like and guides operational- and tactical-level assessments. Strategic planners and evaluators pull together information from other echelons to develop a holistic understanding of their commands' missions and effects.

With regard to SC, USARPAC has a theater-wide view of strategic effects, staffing opportunities and constraints, and relationships with individual country teams that can provide insight into the strength of the United States' relationships with partner countries as well as information on partner countries' objectives. Tactical units executing

SC activities can provide information to help evaluate performance of specific tasks, progress toward SC objectives, and inform understanding of partner country context.

Although USARPAC's strategic evaluation process builds on this doctrinal guidance, it faces key limitations. First, as we discuss below, there is often a lack of conceptual clarity in delineating how USARPAC SC activities contribute to achieving USPACOM campaign objectives. This lack of clarity breaks the linkages that connect the assessment levels shown in Figure 3.2.

Without a clearly understood and specified theory of the causal relationships between SC activities and campaign objectives, it is difficult to identify appropriate measures of effectiveness and performance, or to provide activity executers with sufficient guidance to meet SC objectives effectively. Second, as Figure 3.2 highlights, effective strategic evaluation depends on receiving necessary information from the tactical level. As we discuss in detail in the tactical evaluation section, USARPAC strategic evaluators currently are not receiving sufficient tactical-level information on SC activities.

USARPAC Strategic Evaluation Has Some Shortcomings

USARPAC's strategic evaluation procedure provides a good roadmap for strategic evaluation. As USARPAC planners discussed with our study team and reported to the GAO during its assessment of Pacific Pathways,

> USARPAC conducts a quarterly assessment process in support of achievement of TCSP objectives. This assessment takes into account all activities USARPAC is undertaking to include (TSC) theater security cooperation events. Progress is measured using established Metrics and effects for each Campaign Objective. The results are briefed to the USARPAC Commanding General and his staff and also provided to PACOM in support of their assessment process.[6]

---

[6]   U.S. Army Pacific, "U.S. Army Pacific Response to GAO Questions (GAO 100187 Review of the Army's Pacific Pathways Program, Questions for USARPAC Draft Version 3)," 2015, p. 9.

However, shortcomings in execution limit the effectiveness of its evaluations. Although the process builds in many steps to draw upon cross-echelon monitoring and evaluation, a lack of strategically relevant measures means the evaluation is predominantly driven by senior officers' judgments of partner-nation outcomes. USARPAC has adopted three distinct monitoring and evaluation processes. First, a senior officer (generally an O-6 or above) is assigned as a "manager" for each LOE in USARPAC's TSCP. These managers undertake overarching strategic evaluations of USARPAC's progress toward its SC objectives in their assigned LOEs. Their evaluations are based on their professional military judgment, informed by numerous meetings and planning conferences with partner nations, members of U.S. country teams, and others. Second, USARPAC maintains a PMESII strategic monitoring framework. The PMESII tool enables USARPAC to monitor high-level indicators of trends in its AOR. This tool, however, is simply a monitoring device; it is not designed to explain why things improve, worsen, or remain the same. Finally, USARPAC's SMS is a comprehensive framework that connects specific SC activities with intermediate-level and ultimately campaign-level objectives, and specifies the measures of performance and effectiveness used to monitor progress toward each campaign objective.[7]

In concept, LOE managers draw on material included in SMS, as contextualized by the environmental assessment conducted through PMESII. In practice, LOE managers make very little use of the SMS framework because the information contained in SMS is viewed as low-quality. As an officer responsible for planning commented, "There is currently a disconnect between the intermediate objectives and the specific indicators that show those objectives within the evaluation system . . . . [E]valuations are currently done subjectively, by senior officers, typically USARPAC's LOE managers."[8]

LOE managers do draw upon the PMESII analyses to inform quarterly discussions with senior leaders. However, the PMESII analy-

---

[7]   Our interviews found that USARPAC uses SMS as its SC activities system of record, not G-TSCMIS.

[8]   Interview with USARPAC security cooperation planner, Honolulu, Hawaii, March 3, 2016.

sis cannot fill the gap created by underutilization of SMS. Because SMS is designed as the system of record for USARPAC SC activities, and as such is the knowledge management repository for the cross-echelon assessment framework outlined in Figure 3.2, USARPAC has limited capability to carry out systematic strategic evaluation. By cutting SMS out of the process, LOE managers currently lack an effective, easily accessible and systematic source for recording the relationships between SC activities and campaign objectives, and for capturing metrics and effects.

The Effectiveness of LOE Managers' Judgments Is Affected by the Amount and Quality of the Information They Receive

LOE managers oversee progress toward USPACOM's campaign objectives in each of four USARPAC LOEs: Shape, Posture, Ready, and Communicate. These LOEs cut across USARPAC's campaign objectives, so that the Shape LOE manager is responsible for evaluating progress toward all USPACOM campaign objectives that can be influenced by USARPAC's shaping strategies. LOE managers' responsibilities include oversight of planning, execution, and evaluation of activities that influence their LOE. They lead discussions on their LOE at USARPAC's quarterly senior leaders' meetings. LOE managers' offices are also responsible for updating the measures of effectiveness (MOEs) and measures of performance (MOPs) and for inputting information into SMS. Currently, LOE managers are the most important part of USARPAC's strategic evaluation process. However, if LOE managers receive incomplete information on SC activities, or if the information they do receive is based on poor measures, their evaluations of SC effectiveness may be erroneous or incomplete.

USARPAC Strategic Effects Directorate–Security Cooperation & Policy (FXD-SCP) is the manager for the Shape LOE and is primarily responsible for SC strategic evaluation. FXD-SCP plays a crucial integrating and evaluative role in USARPAC's SC strategic evaluation process. Action officers and the FXD-SCP senior officer interpret disparate information, adjudicate potentially contradictory signals, and collect additional information needed to help in the evaluation process. They use their expertise and understanding of the theater to interpret inputs from SMS and PMESII and develop a more comprehensive evaluation of USARPAC's activities. Any efforts to improve the SMS process will need to be undertaken in close partnership with FXD-SCP.

PMESII Analysis Does Not Link SC Activities to Outcomes in Partner Countries

USARPAC's PMESII model provides a daily updatable, systematic theater environmental analysis. This analysis plays an important role for SC planners by providing macro-level, country-specific information about partner countries. Understanding the non–SC-related factors that influence SC outcomes is important for assessing progress toward strategic objectives.

The PMESII framework is designed to enable multivariate analysis of material drawn from a broad SME network.[9] Each of the model's six dimensions, (political, military, economic, social, information, and infrastructure) is broken down into subdimensions. USARPAC incorporates qualitative and quantitative data from openly available data sources, such as economic data from the World Bank; U.S. government–specific information, such as treaty status; and SME expertise, such as State Department political advisers' judgements, to score countries' achievements on each subdimension. These subdimensions are then aggregated to produce the overarching PMESII scores. In addition to the quantitative analysis, the model includes text-based summary and remarks fields to highlight the most significant effects SMEs identified and provide further clarification of any trends.

The PMESII framework does a good job providing a systematic theater environmental analysis. Our interviews found that many USARPAC personnel involved in planning SC activities used the PMESII framework extensively as a baseline environmental analysis and viewed the PMESII framework as a valuable overview of regional and partner country context necessary for planning. However, because the PMESII framework does not link SC activities to outcomes in partner countries, it cannot be used to evaluate SC activities.

---

[9]   U.S. Army Pacific, "USARPAC Theater Environmental Analysis (Using the PMESII Model)," PowerPoint presentation, limited distribution, April 2015.

SMS Analysis Best When Relationships Between Objectives and Activities Are Well Understood

SMS is built on a hierarchical taxonomy mapping of USPACOM campaign objectives to specific MOEs and MOPs that can be used to evaluate individual activities. Figure 3.3 shows the levels included in SMS. This hierarchy tracks very closely the doctrinal structure presented in Figure 3.1, and is based on the principle that tasks can be causally related to outcomes.

To use SMS effectively, planners need to specify how each task can contribute to progress toward achieving campaign objectives. In our evaluation of activities included in SMS, which we describe in more detail below, we found that the SMS framework did a better job capturing campaign objectives for which the causal relationships between objectives and activities are well understood. In contrast, for campaign objectives for which the causal relationships between objectives and activities are not well understood, it was often difficult to identify how specific activities were expected to contribute to achieving campaign objectives.

Figure 3.3
SMS Hierarchical Taxonomy

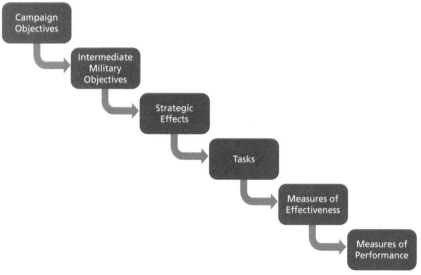

This highlights a perennial challenge for evaluating SC effectiveness. SC objectives are often long-term and frequently not well-defined. Moreover, achieving SC objectives is influenced by many factors other than SC activities. As a result, there is great uncertainty about what works for SC. While recent studies have identified general trends in SC effectiveness, SC planners are often unsure about the causal relationship between SC activities and achievement of campaign objectives.[10] This uncertainty was highlighted across our interviews with personnel at USARPAC and I Corps.

The strengths and weaknesses of the current SMS process are explored in greater depth in the following section. Here, it is sufficient to note that SMS provides a logical, highly structured framework for linking MOEs and MOPs to campaign objectives, closely paralleling the doctrinal evaluation process delineated in JP 3-0 and ADRP 5-0. SMS works well for campaign objectives for which the causal relationships between objectives and activities are well understood and easily measured. Unfortunately, for SC objectives these conditions rarely hold in practice. SMS, as currently implemented, does not do a good job tracking USARPAC's progress toward its objectives when the causal relationships between objectives and activities are less well understood or are difficult to measure. Moreover, our interviews and AAR analyses found that very rarely is tactical-level information included, even though tactical-level information is often the best source for providing MOEs and MOPs.

Summary of Strategic Evaluation Issues

Although there are three elements in USARPAC's strategic evaluation process, the LOE managers are the key component. The PMESII model is valuable for providing a theater environmental analysis, but does not

---

[10] Michael J. McNerney, Angela O'Mahony, Thomas S. Szayna, Derek Eaton, Caroline Baxter, Colin P. Clarke, Emma Cutrufello, Michael McGee, Heather Peterson, Leslie Adrienne Payne and Calin Trenkov-Wermuth, *Assessing Security Cooperation as a Preventive Tool*, Santa Monica, Calif.: RAND Corporation, RR-350-A, 2014; Christopher Paul, Colin P. Clarke, Beth Grill, Stephanie Young, Jennifer D. P. Moroney, Joe Hogler, and Christine Leah, *What Works Best When Building Partner Capacity and Under What Circumstances?* Santa Monica, Calif.: RAND Corporation, MG-1253/1-OSD, 2013.

include information for assessing the outcomes of SC activities. It can be used to evaluate non–SC-related factors that can influence progress toward strategic objectives. Concerns about the information included in SMS have led to SMS being sidelined in USARPAC's strategic evaluation process. Conceptually, SMS provides a rigorous framework that aligns well with joint and Army assessment doctrine, and can lay out the causal logic linking SC activities to strategic objectives. In practice, SMS has numerous weaknesses: it often lacks conceptual clarity, and many of the MOEs and MOPs included in the framework do not appear relevant to measuring progress toward strategic objectives.

As a result, the USARPAC strategic evaluation process is based mainly on the professional judgement of the LOE managers. So long as all stakeholders accept the professional military judgment of the LOE managers, this might not be a problem. But in practice, many other stakeholders—on Capitol Hill and in the Pentagon—do not always accept these judgments.

We believe that the current SMS process is the key gap in USARPAC's strategic evaluation process. Redesigning the SMS system to provide useful information for LOE managers is the most effective change that can be undertaken to improve USARPAC's strategic evaluation process. Below, we present a more detailed discussion of SMS to identify areas for improvement.

SMS: An Illustration of the Limitations of the Current Strategic Evaluation Process

Concerns over the quality of the information included in SMS effectively have led USARPAC to bypass SMS and rely solely on LOE managers' professional judgement and the PMESII environmental assessment. This is problematic because it leads to evaluations of USARPAC SC efforts that are not rigorously linked to information about USARPAC SC activities. Developing a process to increase the value of SMS for USARPAC strategic planners depends upon strengthening the linkages between SC activities and achieving campaign objectives. One approach to doing so is to adopt a "theory of change" process within SMS.

SMS Structure Matches Theory-of-Change Evaluation Approach

Essentially, a theory of change lays out what needs to happen for an activity to contribute to the achievement of an objective, and identifies key milestones to observe along the way. In principle, USARPAC's SMS structure matches well with the theory of change approach to evaluation.[11] This approach has been widely adopted throughout the development community, and is increasingly being used in the defense and security sector.[12] Theories of change connect activities to objectives through causal chains. These causal chains identify the expected results of tasks and specify intermediate steps that can be monitored. For each link in the causal chain, planners specify their assumptions about how subordinate links are related to superordinate links. This allows planners to turn their assumptions into testable hypotheses, and to use these hypotheses to identify measures that can validate these hypotheses.

In an area such as SC, where there is uncertainty about what works, there is often no "right" theory of change. Planners may not be certain of the causal relationships for each link in their causal chain. It is particularly in areas of uncertainty that theories of change are most valuable. By specifying the assumptions that were used to identify activities and their expected links to achieving campaign objectives, evaluation can be used to identify which causal relationships specified in the theory of change are validated over time and which ones need to be changed. Explicit theories of change enable planners to systematically update their understanding of what works for SC. Table 3.1 presents an exploration of common assumptions of how changes in host-nation conditions are often assumed to be improvements, but may also contribute to adverse outcomes. Delineating operations' theories of change and updating them in light with outcome assessments can help planners identify which causal assumptions are accurate and which need to be reconsidered.

---

[11] John Mayne and Nancy Johnson, "Using Theories of Change in the CGIAR Research Program on Agriculture for Nutrition and Health," *Evaluation*, Vol. 21, No. 4, 2015, pp. 407–428.

[12] Jan Osburg, Christopher Paul, Lisa Saum-Manning, Dan Madden, and Leslie Adrienne Payne, *Assessing Locally Focused Stability Operations*, Santa Monica, Calif.: RAND Corporation, RR-387-A, 2014; Andrew Koleros, "Using Theories of Change for Monitoring, Evaluation and Learning," paper presented at Overseas Development Institute's Conference on Theories of Change in International Development, April 7, 2015.

Table 3.1
Assumptions and Potential Alternative Causal Effects or Interpretations

Assumption	Potential Alternative Effect or Interpretation
Development leads to stability.	But it may also lead to increased competition/conflict over the resources made available by development.
Reduction in violence is a positive development.	But it may also indicate complete control of an area by the opposing force.
Roads provide access to markets and health care.	But they may also increase freedom of movement for the opposing force.
Stability must precede development.	But increased development may lead to the desired increase in stability.
Increase in security capacity will reduce violence.	But it can also lead to increased suppression and corruption.
Long-term presence is a key to success.	But it can also foster resentment and/or create dependencies.

SOURCE: Osburg et al., 2014.

Figure 3.4 presents a general theory of change template that matches USARPAC's SMS taxonomy to recommended theory-of-change procedures.[13] This template has three components. First, it lays out the causal chain linking SC activities to campaign objectives. Second, it includes questions that can be used to identify planners' assumptions about how the links in the causal chain are identified and to generate observable measures to evaluate whether these assumptions are valid. The question "Why are activities expected to lead to outputs?" parallels the measures of performance included in SMS. The question "Why are outputs expected to lead to outcomes?" parallels the measures of effectiveness included in SMS. The question "Why are intermediate military objectives expected to lead to campaign objectives?" parallels the strategic effects included in SMS. Third, it includes a question, "Are there other factors that can affect the expected relationships?" that prompts planners to consider what environmental conditions also need to exist for the causal chain to hold, or what environmental conditions would need to change to break the causal chain.

---

[13] This figure is based on Mayne and Johnson, 2015, and tailored to SMS.

Figure 3.4
Theory-of-Change Template for SC

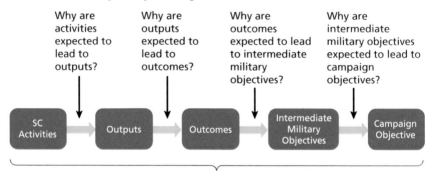

Questions to identify theory of change:

| Why are activities expected to lead to outputs? | Why are outputs expected to lead to outcomes? | Why are outcomes expected to lead to intermediate military objectives? | Why are intermediate military objectives expected to lead to campaign objectives? |

SC Activities → Outputs → Outcomes → Intermediate Military Objectives → Campaign Objective

Are there other factors that can affect the expected relationships?

Figure 3.5 uses this template to work through a notional example linking a training activity to the campaign objective of deterring partner-nation threats. In this example, planners have identified gaps in the partner nation's border surveillance capabilities. By training partner-nation personnel in border surveillance techniques, planners assume that partner-nation personnel will become more proficient at monitoring their border, *and* that the partner nation will utilize its greater surveillance capabilities to increase its border surveillance. Because border surveillance is generally viewed as an important component of border security, greater partner-nation surveillance is expected to contribute to more secure partner-nation borders. Ultimately, more-secure partner-nation borders are assumed to reduce land-based threats to the partner nation.

Potential measures of performance and effectiveness follow from this causal chain. First, U.S. trainers are in a position to assess partner-nation personnel surveillance capabilities following the training event (MOP). However, as training does not always translate into action, monitoring training outputs is necessary but not sufficient. Second, USARPAC planners can have greater confidence in their theory of change (and campaign plan) if they are able to assess whether the partner nation uses its greater capability for border surveillance. A potential MOE for monitoring outcomes is the extent of increased surveil-

Figure 3.5
Theory-of-Change Example: Building Partner Capacity to Deter Threats

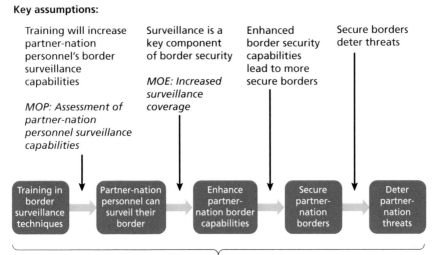

Key assumptions:

| Training will increase partner-nation personnel's border surveillance capabilities | Surveillance is a key component of border security | Enhanced border security capabilities lead to more secure borders | Secure borders deter threats |

MOP: Assessment of partner-nation personnel surveillance capabilities

MOE: Increased surveillance coverage

Training in border surveillance techniques → Partner-nation personnel can surveil their border → Enhance partner-nation border capabilities → Secure partner-nation borders → Deter partner-nation threats

- **Increased regional conflict could increase border threats**
- **Budget cuts for partner-nation military could decrease resources available for border surveillance**

RAND *RR1920-3.5*

lance coverage of the border. USARPAC's ability to monitor outcomes may depend on the strength of its relationship with the partner nation. When the relationship is strong, the partner nation may share this information with USARPAC. When the relationship is weaker, USARPAC may only be able to gain this information indirectly.

Feasible MOPs and MOEs depend on the type of information USARPAC can collect. When relationships with partner nations are strong, Army planners may have greater scope for tracking whether SC activities contribute to achieving their objectives. Army North (ARNORTH) has worked with its partner nations to develop a joint SC planning and assessment process to actively and transparently involve both the United States and the partner nation in assessing how well SC activities contribute to joint objectives.[14]

---

[14] Team member interviews with ARNORTH personnel.

Applying Theories of Change to Activities Included in SMS

We found that across all of the SC-related entries in SMS, the information included in SMS provided a much better roadmap for activities when the causal relationships linking activities and objectives were well-understood and could be influenced by Army efforts. In these cases, activities tended to have well-specified MOPs and MOEs that were clearly related to achieving campaign objectives. Figure 3.6 presents the theory of change for a well-specified partner-nation engagement designed to increase homeland defense.

One of USARPAC's campaign objectives is to integrate USARPAC assets and capabilities with joint and civil authorities to protect against and respond to threats against the United States. Part of USARPAC's communications strategy for homeland defense is to inform partner nations about the United States' homeland defense strategy. There are many benefits to informing partner nations about U.S. homeland defense strategy. First, it reassures partners that the United States will be able to defend itself effectively. Second, it identifies areas in which partners can aid the United States, if necessary. Third, it increases the transparency of U.S. activities in the Pacific. To fulfill its homeland defense communications objectives, USARPAC has planned to undertake communication activities, including discussion of preparedness, joint knowledge awareness systems, and nested response capacity and actions. These topics were identified on the assumption that they will inform partner nations effectively about USARPAC's homeland defense plans. Tracking these events serves as an identifiable MOP that connects well with objectives. Similarly, identifying changes in partner-nation perceptions of USARPAC planning can provide direct insight into whether partner nations understand USARPAC's homeland defense response plan and find it effective. Each of these assumptions and measures of performance and effectiveness were embedded within the SMS entry for this task.

In contrast, when the causal relationships linking activities to objectives are not well-understood or specified, it is difficult to identify effective MOPs and MOEs, and the information recorded in SMS provides a poor roadmap for how to get from activities to the achievement of campaign objectives. Figure 3.7 presents a poorly specified

Figure 3.6
Theory of Change for a Well-Specified USARPAC Partner-Nation Engagement

Links in Causal Chain		Linking Assumptions	Empirical Measures
SC Activity	USARPAC communication activities that include discussion of homeland defense preparedness, joint knowledge awareness systems, nested response capacity, and actions		
		Communications with partner nation will inform partner nation of USARPAC homeland defense plans	• Senior leader engagements with homeland defense discussion • Public information operations, actions, and activities (OAA) with homeland defense discussion • Media engagements with homeland defense discussion
Output	Partner nations are informed about USARPAC homeland defense plans		
		Information about USARPAC homeland defense plans convinces partner nations that homeland defense plans are efficient and effective	Improved perception of USARPAC homeland defense planning
Outcome	Land domain homeland defense response capability requirements identified, appropriately positioned, and prepared to defend against threats		
		Partner nations support USARPAC homeland defense plans	
Intermediate Military Objective	Land domain homeland defense response capability requirements identified, appropriately positioned, and prepared to defend against threats		
		Efficient and effective response capability will enable USARPAC to protect against and respond to threats	
Campaign Objective	USARPAC assets and capabilities are integrated with joint and civil authorities to protect against and respond to homeland threats		

SOURCE: RAND analysis and USARPAC SMS.

RAND RR1920-3.6

causal relationship linking USARPAC partner-nation engagements to strengthening relationships with partner nations.

The campaign objective included in Figure 3.7, "USARPAC strengthens alliances, builds resilient partnerships, and develops multilateral arrangements that share costs, enable agreements, improve regional access, and advance common interests," encompasses most of the goals of the Army's SC strategy. Given the breadth of the campaign objective, it is difficult to specify individual activities that would directly contribute to achieving it. In part, this reflects the reality of SC—USARPAC's overarching relationship with partner nations is the result of all of its engagement, rather than an incremental outcome that can be traced additively to individual events. That said, this approach makes it very difficult to evaluate the effectiveness of individual activities. As Figure 3.7 identifies, planners did not lay out any of the assumptions underlying their beliefs that engagement will strengthen relations with partner nations. Without specific milestones, the MOP and MOE for this causal chain are simple counts of engagements and army-to-army agreed-to actions. Without a theory of change specifying outputs and outcomes that draw on the unique characteristics of individual engagements, evaluators are unable to assess whether any of the events moved USARPAC closer to achieving its objective.

SMS Relies Heavily on Quantitative MOEs and MOPs

Within the SMS framework, evaluations focus on MOEs and MOPs to track progress toward achieving USARPAC campaign objectives. Taken as a whole, the MOEs and MOPs in SMS tend to capture quantities of outcomes and outputs rather than their quality, often using the same or similar measures for MOEs and MOPs. Most metrics appear to be based on the assumption that increased engagement will result in increased capacity. Unfortunately, lessons from SC do not fully support this view.[15] These trends can be seen in Figure 3.8, which lays out USARPAC's Building Partner Capacity campaign objective and associated MOEs and MOPs.

---

[15] McNerney et al., 2014.

Figure 3.7
Theory of Change for a Poorly Specified USARPAC Partner-Nation Engagement

Links in Causal Chain		Linking Assumptions	Empirical Measures
SC Activity	Army engagements with allied personnel		
		Not specified in SMS	Number of Army engagements with allied personnel
Output	Multiple engagements with allied personnel		
		Not specified in SMS	Measure alliance nation's army's desire for army-to-army relationship by assessing generation and approval of army-to-army agreed-to actions
Outcome	Generation and approval of army-to-army agreed-to actions		
		Not specified in SMS	
Intermediate Military Objective	By FY 2020, alliances are enhanced, perceptions of U.S. commitment and access are increased, and relationships which improve regional security are developed and strengthened		
		Interaction between USARPAC and ally armies sends strong message of cooperation and resolve to potential adversaries	
Campaign Objective	USARPAC strengthens alliances, builds resilient partnerships, and develops multilateral arrangements that share costs, enable agreements, improve regional access, and advance common interests		

SOURCE: RAND analysis and USARPAC SMS.

RAND RR1920-3.7

As Figure 3.8 highlights, most of the MOEs and MOPs included in SMS for Building Partner Capacity activities rely on numerical inputs: counts of events, exercises, OAAs, agreed-to actions, funding requests, requests for USARPAC elements, and requests for activity sets. Overreliance on quantitative metrics is a common problem in almost all evaluation frameworks, and has led to a critique that evaluations increase attention on activities that are more measureable, to the detriment of activities that may be more important but are more difficult to quantify.[16] It is also a concern recognized by USARPAC training material for campaign assessments. A briefing for personnel involved in developing intermediate objectives notes that the goal is "quality of metrics, not quantity. If [metrics are] easy to measure, [they are] probably not a good MOE."[17] We believe reliance on easy-to-measure, but not particularly relevant, quantitative metrics is often exacerbated in the SMS process by the lack of conceptual clarity in the causal relationship linking SC activities to strategic objectives.

Quantitative measures are often perceived as more objective, more rigorous, and easier to collect than qualitative measures. However, if quantitative measures do not capture the relationships that matter for evaluating progress toward objectives, their precision provides false comfort. It is more useful to rely on potentially subjective, noncomparable qualitative measures instead of the wrong quantitative measures, as long as evaluators understand how the qualitative measures are generated. Alternatively, for SC activities that are strategically important, entail causal relationships that are conceptually uncertain, and are conducted with partners committed to working with the United States, USARPAC can implement impact evaluations to more rigorously test specific propositions.

---

[16] Arie Halachmi, "Performance Measurement Is Only One Way of Managing Performance," *International Journal of Productivity and Performance Management*, Vol. 54, No. 7, 2005, pp. 502–516; Donald P. Moynihan, *The Dynamics of Performance Management: Constructing Information and Reform*, Washington, D.C.: Georgetown University Press, Public Management and Change Series, 2008.

[17] Chris Bachl and Molly Kihara, "USARPAC Metrics in Support of Campaign Assessment," presentation to USARPAC, March 12, 2014.

Figure 3.8
Measures to Evaluate Progress Toward Building Partner Capacity

---

Building Partner Capacity Campaign Objective

Develop and enhance partnership capacity to (a) address drivers of instability; (b) deny terrorist safe havens and disrupt their ability to plan, resource, and conduct attacks; (c) defend against and respond to a weapons of mass destruction (WMD) attack; (d) prevent the proliferation of WMD material, expertise, and delivery systems; (e) secure border and defeat conventional threats; and (f) respond to all hazards events.

Measures of Effectiveness

Quantitatively Oriented Measures
- Number of partner engagement OAAs executed with partner nations on drivers of instability, denying safe havens, conducting counter WMD, securing borders, and responding to all-hazard events
- Number of agreed to actions where one or more partner country program abilities are trained
- Number of 1206 and 1207 funding requests for partner nations by USARPAC
- Increased requests for USARPAC elements
- Partner nations request land-based, dual-use Army prepositioned stock (APS) activity sets

Qualitatively Oriented Measures
- USARPAC solidifies agreements (missile defense, intelligence sharing, cyber, logistical) where forward deployed in partner nation
- Increase in partner nations' perception of USARPAC's ability to develop and strengthen regional security
- Measure of the quality of land domain participation in exercises to assess increased interoperability
- Increased data sharing between partner nations and land component commander

---

Measures of Performance

Quantitatively Oriented Measures
- Number of partner nations that show increased desire/participation for joint or combined events that address drivers of instability, denying safe havens, conducting counter-WMD, securing borders, and responding to all-hazard events
- Number of agreed to actions where one or more partner country program abilities are trained
- Total number of multilateral exercises
- Number of partner nations that participate in a USARPAC-sponsored 1206 and 1207 engagement event or demonstration
- Percentage of available land-based, dual-use APS that are used by Pacific Pathways (and/or other U.S. land domain units) and partner nations during training events
- USARPAC invited to participate in activities (e.g., logistical, operational, institutional, humanitarian) that support persistent engagement
- USARPAC communication OAAs with partner nations that include discussion of interoperability between USARPAC and land domain elements
- USARPAC executes WMD elimination, hazard events, counterterrorism training and all-hazard training events that support partner-nation requests

Qualitatively Oriented Measures
- USARPAC develops, integrates, and provides Human Terrain Mapping data in support of partner nation capabilities
- USARPAC positions dual purpose activity sets
- USARPAC develops training strategies to support partner nations' training requirements

---

SOURCE: RAND analysis and USARPAC SMS.

RAND *RR1920-3.8*

Impact Evaluations Can Provide Rigorous Assessments

Impact evaluations assess changes (generally at the individual or community level) in particular outcomes (such as individual behavior or community characteristics) that can be attributed to a specific activity (such as a particular program or activity). Impact evaluations are based conceptually on testing a counterfactual—what would have occurred in the absence of the program or activity. The importance of assessing the counterfactual differentiates impact evaluations from more general monitoring and evaluation activities that base their assessment on descriptions only of what happened where the programs or activities were implemented (e.g., the factual). Testing the counterfactual generally requires identifying a context in which the program or activity was not implemented that is almost identical to the one in which the program or activity was implemented, and measuring the differences in outcomes between them.[18]

For the past several years, the international development community has been conducting impact evaluations to evaluate programs designed to improve outcomes. Unfortunately, there has been much less attention focused on impact evaluations on security-related programs.[19]

Three points in particular stand out from development-oriented impact evaluations. First, in some cases they yield counterintuitive results. Programs that had been effective in one context turned out to be ineffective in another. Practitioners relying on "lessons learned" were often applying the wrong lessons.[20] As a result, impact evaluations serve as a valuable tool to help planners reexamine their initial assumptions and to identify which causal links actually work.

---

[18]   Committee on Evaluation of USAID Democracy Assistance Programs, *Improving Democracy Assistance: Building Knowledge Through Evaluations and Research*, Washington, D.C.: National Academies Press, 2008.

[19]   Drew B Cameron, Annette N. Brown, Anjini Mishra, Mario Picon, Hisham Esper, Flor Calvo, and Katia Peterson, *Evidence for Peacebuilding: An Evidence Gap Map*, New Delhi: International Initiative for Impact Evaluation, Evidence Gap Map Report 1, April 2015.

[20]   For example, Andrew Radin has written that supposed lessons from Bosnia were misapplied to the contemporary case of Syria. See "The Misunderstood Lessons of Bosnia for Syria," *Washington Quarterly*, Vol. 37, No. 4, 2015, pp. 55–69.

Second, impact evaluations are often structured in such a way as to examine multiple possible interventions and do so with considerable nuance. Instead of simply identifying whether a program "worked" or "didn't work," many of the studies were able to suggest which specific approaches were best and most cost effective. Indeed, this second point is related to the first. Some of the academics conducting these studies were able to learn from early failures and work with local implementing partners to adapt policies in ways that ultimately yielded success. This approach can provide an extremely valuable iterative evaluation process for USARPAC's longer-term SC activities, such as building partner capacity.

Third, successful impact evaluations require buy-in from local communities. Impact evaluations tend to occur when both partners are invested in improving the quality of the program or activity being assessed. For SC, this means that impact evaluations should be considered part of a joint evaluation process in which both USARPAC and the partner nation are involved in SC planning and assessment activities. Joint planning and assessment process will not be feasible for all SC activities or with all partners. However, it is a viable option with many U.S. partners. ARNORTH has begun developing a joint SC planning and assessment structure that can serve as a model for USARPAC.[21]

Impact evaluations hold the potential to improve USARPAC's conduct of SC activities and to steer resources to the most cost-effective capabilities and operations. They can provide a rigorous assessment for activities that are difficult to assess with other assessment processes and for which it is particularly important to understand how effective USARPAC SC activities are. It is nonetheless important not to overstate the potential of impact evaluations. They are a complex and demanding form of evaluation, and they will not be appropriate in many circumstances, such as one-off small unit exchanges.

Impact evaluations should not be viewed as an assessment strategy to adopt for every SC activity. As such, we believe that they should be used very selectively to supplement professional military judgment on certain key questions. Investing in impact evaluations makes the most

---

[21]   Interview with officers in Houston, Texas, January 5, 2016.

sense for SC activities that are strategically important, entail causal relationships that are   conceptually uncertain, and are conducted with partners committed to working with the United States

Understanding Causal Relationships Better Can Improve Strategic Evaluation

Overall, this illustration of the SMS process serves to demonstrate that USARPAC's LOE managers' concerns over the quality of information included in SMS is well-founded. The causal chains linking SC activities to strategic objectives tend to be poorly specified, and the MOEs and MOPs tend to be difficult to reconcile with USARPAC's strategic objectives. This is unfortunate, as (in principle) the SMS framework could enable a strategic evaluation process that is more in keeping with joint and Army guidance on conducting strategic evaluations. Improving the causal chains and metrics included in SMS can help improve USARPAC's strategic evaluation process.

Potential Improvements in Strategic Evaluation

USARPAC's strategic evaluation process is well-designed conceptually, but it has some key weaknesses as currently implemented. The current process relies heavily on senior officers' professional judgements. LOE managers are constrained in their strategic assessment efforts by poor information on how well USARPAC SC activities are performing and the lack of a rigorous analysis of how SC activities are designed to accomplish USARPAC's strategic objectives.

USARPAC's SMS process, which is designed to provide information on the effectiveness of SC activities for achieving strategic objectives, is plagued by a lack of conceptual clarity and a   dearth of high-quality MOEs and MOPs. LOE managers do find that the PMESII framework provides valuable environmental assessments. However, as these are not formally incorporated into planners' expectations of how environmental conditions may affect the likelihood that SC activities can contribute to strategic objectives, it is unclear whether the information included in   PMESII is providing the right information.

Figure 3.9 presents a process map for an improved strategic evaluation process. Figure 3.9 includes the three main components of USARPAC's strategic evaluation process—LOE managers, PMESII, and

SMS. LOE managers are responsible for strategic evaluation. They draw on information provided through the PMESII and SMS frameworks.

Two key changes from the current system are specified in this process map. First, USARPAC planners adopt theories of change as a part of the planning process. Theories of change will help planners identify strategic effects, intermediate military objectives and SC activities, and their concomitant MOEs and MOPs that are assumed to be causally linked to strategic objectives.

Clearly specified theories of change will also aid evaluators to identify when hypothesized causal relationships received support through the collected MOEs and MOPs. If there is no support for the hypothesized causal relationships, then they can be updated. USARPAC's ERPs for priority countries, which include three- and five-year plans for USARPAC's OAA slates, provide a good opportunity for the reevaluation of the theories of change underlying USARPAC's engagement strategies with their priority partners.

Second, the process map in Figure 3.6 highlights the importance of incorporating tactical-level information into USARPAC's strategic evaluation process. This is a key point that we return to in Chapter Four.

Figure 3.9
USARPAC Strategic Evaluation Process Map

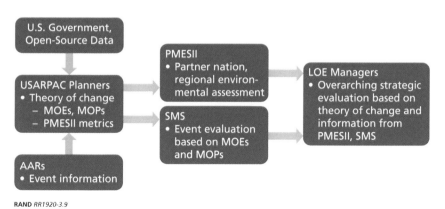

RAND *RR1920-3.9*

Tactical Evaluation

Tactical evaluation enables executing units to determine whether they have fulfilled stated mission objectives, learned from an event, and shared that learning with other units. This process is conducted through AARs. The primary focus of AARs is to capture lessons learned during an event and improve overall unit performance; traditionally, AARs do not focus on collecting information on environment, strategic goals, or end states.

The next section describes the current doctrine and guidance for tactical units, followed by an analysis of 19 AARs from SC events executed by Army units in the USPACOM AOR. The analysis examines the content and usefulness of the AARs in both the tactical and strategic contexts. We conclude with recommendations to improve the information collected from tactical executors and suggestions to improve the AAR format and organize information to make it more useful to mission executors.

Current Doctrine and Guidance Flows from Two Primary Sources

Several doctrinal publications govern how the military (and the Army in particular) gathers information from events, validates its accuracy, leverages observations, integrates them to be adapted and applied by other units, and conducts assessments during implementation to see whether corrections need to be made.[22] Two primary documents govern doctrine at the joint level: the "Joint Lessons Learned Program" (which governs the processes for capturing and disseminating lessons for the joint force) and the "Lessons Learned Collection Efforts from Military Operation" memorandum.[23] These documents provide the framework for Army Lessons Learned doctrine.

---

[22] Army Regulation 11-33, *Army Lessons Learned Program*, Washington, D.C.: Headquarters, Department of the Army, October 17, 2006, p. 3-1.

[23] Chairman of the Joint Chiefs of Staff Instruction 3150.25C, "Joint Lessons Learned Program," Washington, D.C.: Office of the Chairman of the Joint Chiefs of Staff, 2007; Chairman of the Joint Chiefs of Staff, "Lessons Learned Collection Efforts for Military Operations," Washington, D.C., Memorandum for Chiefs of the Military Services, CM-0028-14, February 4, 2014.

Army Lessons Learned Program and AARs Not Specific for SC Events

Army Regulation 11-33, *Army Lessons Learned Program*, mandates the collection and dissemination of Army lessons, insights, and tactics, techniques, and procedures; establishes the Lessons Learned program; and designates the Center for Army Lessons Learned (CALL) as the repository for all lessons learned. The regulation states

> Commanding generals (CGs) of all Army commands, ASCCs, and direct reporting units (DRUs) will . . . direct assigned units, brigade-sized or larger (except in the case of specialty units which operate/deploy separately at the platoon, company, or battalion levels), to submit unit-level AARs and other lessons learned material to CALL for review, analysis, dissemination, and archiving.[24]

It further goes on to specify that AARs are to be submitted to CALL within 90 days after returning to home station after participating in an Army, joint, or combined military operation and no later than 60 days after returning to home station after participating in an Army, joint, or combined training exercise or experiment.[25]

While this guidance mandates the submission of AARs to CALL, it is not as specific as it needs to be for SC activities. Many of the units executing these activities are small teams, squads, and platoons from DRUs. Army Regulation 11-33 does not specifically require these smaller elements to report AARs to CALL or direct collection into another AAR repository. At the time of writing, a new version of Army Regulation 11-33 was awaiting formal approval; this version calls for CGs, ASCCs, and DRUs to "ensure that a lessons learned capability that facilitates discovery, validation, integration and assessment is embedded in all commands and activities."[26] It further mandates CGs, ASCCs, and DRUs to

---

[24] Army Regulation 11-33, 2006, p. 2-3.

[25] Army Regulation 11-33, 2006.

[26] Army Regulation 11-33, *Army Lessons Learned Program (ALLP)*, Washington, D.C.: Headquarters, Department of the Army, draft, undated, p. 2-3. Not available to the public.

[e]ngage unified action partner to determine willingness, capability, and capacity to exchange information and establish data sharing procedures such as seminars, workshops, multinational engagements, partner exercises, bilateral staff talks, and so on.[27]

This change puts the onus on each command and activity to maintain a lessons-learned capability, actively search for partner-nation inputs, and maintain the collected information.

FM 6-0, *Commander and Staff Organization and Operations*, devotes an entire chapter to the AAR process, describes the methodology and guidance to conduct the process, and provides an AAR template that elaborates on the process.[28] Accurate reporting of events through AARs is a critical part of the evaluation process, necessary to capture lessons learned and foster improved performance.

As lessons and recommendations emerge from mission executors, they need to be captured and fed back into the planning process. The focus for these reports varies at each level: Mission executors focus on improving their processes and performance; corps and division headquarters focus on successful mission completion and improving unit readiness; and ASCCs focus on how the mission contributes to TSCP objectives. Reports must include specific objectives (with corresponding measures) for the event, and information from the AAR must be shared across the command so that recommendations can be incorporated into staff processes to update future operations.

In practice, few of these guidelines are followed. As best as we could determine, very few SC-related AARs are submitted to CALL. Moreover, most of these AARs focus solely on improving performance at the tactical level and rarely address issues of concern for planners at higher headquarters. The following analysis demonstrates in greater detail the disconnect between reported information and required information, specifically as it relates to I Corps and USARPAC outputs and outcomes.

---

[27] Army Regulation 11-33, undated.

[28] FM 6-0, 2014.

AARs Fail to Provide as Much Critical Information as They Should

To understand how AARs worked in practice, we attempted to acquire every AAR available from Army-executed SC events in the USPACOM AOR. To locate these AARs, we sent requests to every centralized repository of AARs and lessons-learned programs, including CALL, the Joint Center for International Security Force Assistance, the Joint Lessons Learned Information System, and the Asymmetric Warfare Group. We also made numerous inquiries of USARPAC and Army units operating in the USPACOM AOR.

Despite every effort to identify as many AARs as possible, we were able to locate only 19 AARs. Notwithstanding the relatively small sample size, we believe that these AARs fairly represent in-theater AARs more broadly. They contain information on events involving a broad spectrum of activities and conducted with a variety of partner nations. The events described ranged in size from small-team SME exchanges to battalion-sized activities linked to Pacific Pathways.

After acquiring the AARs, we analyzed their content, their storage and dissemination, and their use by relevant stakeholders.[29] We found that current AARs fail to provide as much critical feedback as they should on both event execution and the accomplishment of strategic-level goals. They also fail to capture information about partner forces that would assist future planning efforts. Storage and dissemination problems mean that the insights that AARs do provide do not find their way to a large audience. Finally, even if AARs were routinely conducted, stored, and disseminated effectively, strategic evaluation processes are not configured to make good use of AAR content.

AARs Lack Critical Feedback

AARs can be useful at two levels. At the tactical level, AARs can help event planners improve execution. At the strategic level, AARs can be one source of data to evaluate strategic SC effects and adjust planning accordingly. Perhaps unsurprisingly, AARs conducted by tactical-level units executing SC events almost exclusively focus on tactical functions—but even here, AARs provide much less critical feedback than they should.

---

[29] For a full list of categories and subcategories, see Appendix A.

We analyzed whether the 19 AARs provided critical feedback on SC event planning, execution, and effectiveness and whether they made suggestions about future activities. As Figure 3.10 indicates, only four of the 19 AARs addressed all four of these areas; three addressed some, but not all, of these areas; and 12 did not provide critical commentary in any area.

Part of the problem may be that those who conducted the AARs did not use standardized criteria. None of the AARs mentioned explicit MOPs or MOEs tied to the lines of operation specified in mission orders or other guidance from higher headquarters.

The Army culture of learning emphasizes focusing on "tasks, conditions, and standards" when conducting instruction. The "task" is the activity that must be accomplished, the "conditions" are the environment, and the "standards" are the level of performance that needs to be met. However, "performance" and "effectiveness" are entirely different metrics. A unit is unlikely to use these metrics because they are not in common grading rubrics and are specific to each mission. The failure to even mention evaluation systems or reporting metrics in many of

Figure 3.10
Proportion of AARs Providing In-Depth Critique of U.S. Performance

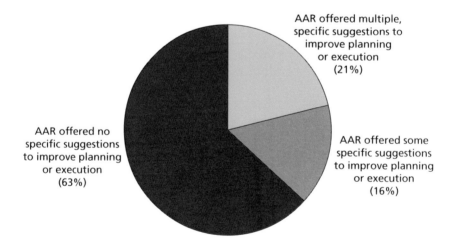

AARs indicates that mission executors lack the tools to think critically about mission success at the strategic level.

A small number of the analyzed AARs, however, provided extremely useful critical feedback, and these offer insights into how other AARs could be improved. One such AAR was from a Philippine SME exchange. This AAR discussed a road map to establish priorities that would create a Philippine capability. It explained partner-nation and U.S. efforts to meet that end state and provided a detailed discussion of the event. It established LOEs for the event and provided day-by-day descriptions to show how those LOEs were accomplished. Finally, it gave concrete next steps for the Philippine Army and U.S. forces to take to build that capability.

AARs Fail to Capture Information on Foreign Security Forces

Analysis revealed that only three of the 19 AARs adequately captured information on partner-nation security forces. Specifically, these AARs contained information on the capabilities a partner brought into an event, how these capabilities developed during the event, and recommendations for possible future missions. Collecting metrics on foreign security forces is widely acknowledged to be a contentious subject, and perceptions that U.S. forces are "grading" a partner nation or collecting intelligence should be avoided. Rather, partner-nation capabilities should be viewed through a capability-development lens. The more U.S. units know about partner-nation units, the more accurately they can tailor future missions.

Establishing a baseline for future U.S. SC activities and missions is critical to gaining this knowledge. While PMESII looks at the strategic environment, there are no metrics to evaluate specific partner-nation units. This drastically hinders the long-term ability of U.S forces to build rapport and relations with partner nations. Developing such a baseline could help strategic-level planners and evaluators measure progress and plan next steps and tactical-level executors better calibrate planning to partner capabilities and needs.

The extent to which executing units collect information on partner-nation security forces is likely to be determined by U.S. relations with the partner. As noted in the section on strategic evaluations, other geographic combatant commands have entered into collaborative evaluations with certain close partners. In these cases, both the United States and the partner work closely together to assess progress across a variety of dimensions, using explicit metrics. Where the United States lacks such close relations, information gathering will necessarily be much more minimal. But even in these cases, executing units cannot help but notice issues, such as interoperability concerns. Formally recording such observations after an event is complete should not imperil partnerships; rather, it should provide the basis for more-fruitful cooperation in future iterations of these events.

Complicating the matter is the USARPAC battle rhythm and planning process, which directs when and how exercise objectives must be agreed to with partner nations. The Joint Event Life Cycle locks in U.S. training commitments far in advance of an SC activity; when partner-nation objectives change, often little can be done to alter the activity until soldiers arrive at the event.[30] While some (mostly small-scale) events occur outside the Joint Event Life Cycle, most larger events occur within the cycle and are subject to its time frame requirements. Additionally, many foreign security forces will pull from multiple units to create a partnering element. This is often done so that the individuals who receive the training can go back to their own units and share the lessons that U.S. forces provided. However, the general lack of knowledge about partner-nation forces limits U.S. forces and how they plan for a mission. For example, it makes little sense to train basic soldier skills to an advanced unit that is more interested in noncommissioned officer development. Without a baseline of partner-nation capabilities, it is hard to provide specific, well-focused training.

Nonetheless, with partner-nation agreement and cooperation, executing units would be able to collect data that are necessary to measure capability changes over time. Ensuring that this type of information is included in AARs would help tailor more-effective missions.

---

[30] Interview with officers in Honolulu, Hawaii, November 4–6, 2015.

Knowledge Management Does Not Document or Disseminate Individual Information

Virtually all Army units conduct an AAR upon completion of a mission. Unfortunately, all too often, insufficient knowledge management means this information does not go beyond the executing unit or the next higher echelon, and SC AARs are almost nonexistent in CALL and the Joint Lessons Learned Information System. The AARs we analyzed rarely followed a standard template and varied considerably in size and amount of information. This lack of standardization (e.g., some AARs were organized by functional topic and others by chronology) allows maximum flexibility, but it is problematic for anyone trying to aggregate information quickly. The process of comparing AAR information quickly becomes onerous because of these variations, and any systematic approach is difficult. The problem is the same for tactical executors trying to learn from previous unit activities as for strategic planners looking for information that has strategic implications. In part because AARs are not widely disseminated, information from tactical units is rarely incorporated into USARPAC's strategic evaluations, denying planners critical information.

I Corps has instituted a knowledge management plan to capture and document tactical knowledge and ensure its dissemination. However, while this plan describes many of the business processes necessary for the command to function, it is not rigorously followed or enforced, particularly for AARs and evaluations. In reference to the I Corps repository, one interviewee stated that "every relevant SC AAR is available," but several other interviewees reported that, while all AARs were posted onto the I Corps web portal, AARs that were more than one-and-a-half years old were permanently deleted, and AARs for smaller events were not systematically updated or maintained.[31] Numerous interviewees from USARPAC, I Corps, and DRUs stated that AARs were routinely conducted for SC activities and that they were collected into a repository. We searched many of these repositories for this study, including CALL, the Joint Center for International Security

---

[31] Interview with officers in Joint Base Lewis McChord, Washington, November 11–13, 2015.

Force Assistance, I Corps, and 25 Infantry Division (ID) repositories. The USARPAC Share Point portal server is the logical place to put Army AARs from the Pacific theater, yet many interviewees stated they had difficulty accessing this site (the RAND team could not access it, despite numerous attempts). Even major subordinate commands often do not have access to information on the site; this inaccessible information includes general officer executive summaries of trips to partner nations.[32]

The I Corps Share Point portal server or, possibly, G-TSCMIS could act as a repository for AARs if access to the USARPAC site remains constrained. However, they are not ideal for long-term AAR storage. Issues such as constrained server capacity, staff turnover, and other competing priorities increase the likelihood that AARs will be misplaced or erased on a regular basis. Therefore, tactical units should preferably archive their AARs both at USARPAC and at an Army central repository, such as CALL.

An additional constraint on locating AARs is the lack of a standard naming convention or easy-to-use search functions on the repository sites, both of which reduce the likelihood of finding relevant AARs.

Because of limits in access to the above-mentioned AAR repositories, the most common way of procuring an AAR is through point-to-point communication. While such an approach is convenient and circumvents some of the knowledge management issues discussed above, it only provides insights from one unit, doing one event, with one partner, at one point in time. It therefore limits planners' ability to compare insights across multiple AARs. While some interviewees stated that AARs were being created and were available for planners and executors who knew where to look, most often the only available AAR was from the previous year's event; attempts to locate previous AARs were often unsuccessful. Sometimes, an AAR identified a person or office to contact for comments or questions, which aided in the location of additional AARs, but this was not always the case. Having a way to contact the AAR's author or approver is critical to planners and exec-

---

[32] Interview with officers in Honolulu, Hawaii, November 4–6, 2015.

utors who have follow-up questions or comments, especially because the start of the planning process—mission analysis—begins with the review of past AARs.

Another issue affecting knowledge management is continuity and communication between personnel, units, and partner nations. Military personnel at USARPAC, I Corps, and division level rotate constantly. As a result, it is difficult to maintain any kind of continuity between planners, many of whom are frequently pulled from primary planning duty to assist in other, more-pressing requirements. Often multiple personnel rotate into the primary planning position for an SC event. Those who attended early planning events are unlikely to be the ones involved in event execution. In one case, *four* planners rotated through the same critical staff position before the event they each had helped to plan took place.[33] While units are trying to implement standard operating procedures so that information is not lost when staff officers rotate, these efforts have not eliminated the underlying challenges. For mission executors, the problem is highlighted when the primary staff officer for mission-specific questions is new to the job and unaware of the mission specifics. The realignment of directorates at USARPAC and I Corps has added to the confusion caused by personnel rotation. As both go through reorganizations and downsize, it is often unclear which directorates should be discussing SC events and in what time frame. For mission executors, this often translates into little guidance outside the formal order. Many of the problems related to personnel churn are inherent in the Army personnel management system. Although the underlying challenge cannot be resolved by either ASCCs or units, the problems can be greatly mitigated by effective knowledge management practices.

Linking AARs to Strategic Evaluations

The lack of tactical information in the evaluation process is an important shortfall in USARPAC operations. To improve evaluation, information from unit executors needs to be incorporated into the SMS evaluation system. Multiple senior USARPAC officials acknowledged

---

[33] Interview with officers in Honolulu, Hawaii, November 4–6, 2015.

that feedback from AARs and evaluations is not being incorporated into the process loop, and one SC professional noted the lack of "formal processes" to incorporate feedback from the units executing SC events.[34] Without this feedback loop, substantial information from activities does not get incorporated into planning. Information from mission executors gives firsthand knowledge on the activities, training, conditions, and interoperability of foreign security forces. This information is vital for evaluators to build strong causal links to create effective MOEs and MOPs that link tactical activities to theater goals, and ultimately to assess whether SC activities contributed to capability development. U.S. defense attachés and SC officers involved in these events provide some of this information. Such officials, however, lack the depth of tactical-level interaction that executing units gain.

Conclusion

This chapter analyzed the SC evaluation process at USARPAC and at tactical levels. There is a tremendous amount of activity in the Pacific region, yet it is difficult to determine how much these activities are contributing to theater goals and objectives. The outcomes from SC events are not well understood, and linking tactical tasks to strategic end states in a logical manner is a goal not yet attained. The evaluation tools and processes currently in place have the ability to capture inputs, outputs, and outcomes, but they need additional information. Improvements to strategic evaluation should focus on improving the systems currently in place, adopting a theory of change to improve clarity, ensuring that MOEs and MOPs are clearly aligned with intermediate military objectives, and leveraging impact evaluations to supplement the evaluation process. At the tactical level, critical information is missing from unit-level AARs. Units should focus on improving the quality of information they provide to ensure that it is relevant for planners and evaluators, working with partner-nation security forces to

---

[34] Interview with officers in Honolulu, Hawaii, November 4–6, 2015.

help establish a baseline of knowledge for individual units, and ensuring that AARs are submitted and stored in the appropriate repository.

SC activities are an investment intended to improve U.S. national security by building the capacity of allies and partners. Like many investments, it is difficult to predict how well SC will pay off. Like any wise investor, USARPAC and I Corps should monitor and assess the results of their efforts to help decide what to continue doing and what to change.

CHAPTER FOUR

Conclusion and Recommendations

Security cooperation is an inherently complex and challenging activity. The processes USARPAC, I Corps, and subordinate commands currently use to manage those challenges generally function at least adequately and often well. This report has sought to identify where those processes might be improved and offer concrete suggestions for improvements. Most of these suggestions represent a potential for incremental progress, building on what already works and the knowledge and skills of those currently managing these efforts. None of these suggestions is costless.[1] Consequently, the research team offers them as options for consideration, recognizing that resourcing constraints may prevent some of them from being implemented.

The recommendations fall into two categories: recommendations for improvements in planning and recommendations for improvements in evaluation. Both entail concomitant improvements in coordination processes.

---

[1] A topic for future research might be an assessment of the relative level of resources required to execute each of our recommendations. Such a project could consider resources (e.g., staffing, funding, and time) to produce an estimate of the level of effort required for execution.

Recommendations for USARPAC and I Corps Planning: Strategic/Operational-Level Recommendations

USARPAC Should Clarify Readiness and Security Cooperation Objectives

USARPAC and its subordinate units conduct most SC activities through events that also improve unit readiness. We noted earlier that an ongoing debate exists within subordinate headquarters regarding which set of objectives have or should have priority. This is partly a legal and fiscal issue beyond the scope of this study. However, we posited that due to statutory restrictions on the use of many types of funds used for SC activities, unit readiness will often be the priority. As the aviation SC event discussion made clear, SC events can be used to pursue both readiness and shaping goals, but some trade-offs are involved. These trade-offs include the amount of planners' time spent on one or the other, the amount of training time spent on cross-cultural communications skills rather than warfighting skills, and the amount of time spent during the SC event on social activities designed to build rapport rather than technical military capacity building.

This is an issue of strategic guidance. USARPAC should consider promulgating default guidance (perhaps through the USARPAC command training guidance) stating that, in the absence of event-specific direction, both types of objectives should be equally pursued, yet when they are in conflict, unit readiness comes first. This could ensure that tactical units—which might otherwise give negligible time and attention to TSC/shaping goals—move toward greater balance when conducting a large exercise or other SC event.

USARPAC and I Corps should also provide more comprehensive guidance on objectives when drafting the orders for specific SC activities. The earlier discussion of strategic objectives highlighted dilemmas and potential conflicts between objectives that might be faced by a small U.S. aviation maintenance team sent to work with a partner aviation unit. While the specifics of those dilemmas pertain to that particular event, they also highlight more general ways that differing objectives could potentially conflict during execution of an SC activity. To provide guidance on these potential conflicts, USARPAC and

I Corps should consider addressing the following issues, as appropriate, in the commander's intent section of operations orders:

- Should capacity building efforts focus on short-term or long-term capacity building needs (e.g., "quick wins" or efforts that will require repeated efforts over years)?
- How important is interoperability as a goal of the engagement? Where interoperability is a priority, what type, level, or scope of interoperability is required?
- What priority should be placed on relationship building? (If this is the first engagement of a series of engagements to be conducted over a multi-year period, rapport and relationship-building might be the priority. If the United States has been working with a specific partner force or unit for a considerable time, the achievement of certain technical goals might outweigh building rapport.)
- How much effort should the executing unit spend on maintaining its own readiness (understood primarily in terms of traditional warfighting functions) versus building partner capacity?
- Are there any secondary objectives?

Provide Information So Units Understand Commander's Intent

Units involved in SC events do not always possess the information they need to execute the commander's intent. In particular, two types of information should more consistently flow from higher headquarters to tactical units. First, tactical units often lack critical background informationon partner-nation goals and priorities. Executive summaries from high-level engagements that set out the goals for SC events are a key resource that could help to correct this problem. They should be more widely distributed, while recognizing some elements may be sensitive and need to be redacted before wide distribution. Second, higher headquarters should invest more effort in developing and disseminating strategic communications themes for SC. Interviewees reported that USARPAC disseminates periodic SC talking points, but this guidance is not clearly linked to specific events. As a result, leaders for SC events are often provided only extremely vague guidance about themes they should emphasize in communications with partners.

Sustain Multiechelon Involvement in Planning

Interviewees consistently reported that participation in selected higher-echelon planning activities enabled parallel planning, improved vertical communication and coordination, and provided forums to pose questions and gain additional information more quickly and effectively than formal requests for information. Authoritative memorandum or other summaries should be produced and distributed from each of these events so that everyone is working from the same understanding. As noted earlier, not everyone comes out of the same meeting with a common understanding of what was decided, and authoritative records of those conversations can help prevent participants from heading down different roads afterward.

Recommendations for USARPAC and I Corps Planning: Tactical-Level Recommendations

Create Accessible Country Folders

We recommend that USARPAC develop a knowledge management system that provides subordinate headquarters with information designed to provide a comprehensive planning, coordination, and evaluation resource to a unit executing an SC activity in the USPACOM area of responsibility (including checklists, forms, and contact data). These could be as simple as a set of folders organized by partner nation and housed within the USARPAC portal under the Security Cooperation Policy Division. These folders could include a generic checklist of SC activities alongside other general guidance documents. The appendixes contain suggested checklists and formats. Some of this information overlaps with the data required in G-TSCMIS. Ideally, in such cases USARPAC could automate its processes so that both the USARPAC portal and G-TSCMIS would automatically be updated as more recent information becomes available. In many other cases, the information required by tactical-level units has no corresponding field in G-TSCMIS, in which case the USARPAC portal would be the authoritative source of information.

Country subfolders could be actively managed by the corresponding desk officers in the SCP division; each country folder would contain information relevant for planners as they prepare for an SC activity (see Figure 4.1).

At a minimum, individual country folders should contain a variety of information specific to executing an SC event in a country. Many interviewees for this report stated that logistics and administrative actions were the largest   hurdles to executing an SC event. As each country has different processes for entrance, a clearly delineated process should be posted, along with the corresponding forms for access.

Clearing customs is equally difficult, posting the correct forms could prevent a lot of confusion. Communications information would also be helpful for planners, including points of contact for questions; emails and phone numbers; and details on obtaining and executing funding, medical readiness, force protection, and evaluations within each country's borders. Generic information that applies to all or most partner nations could be cut and pasted into each folder to provide "one-stop shopping" for tactical-level planners. This information might

Figure 4.1
Example of Country Folder

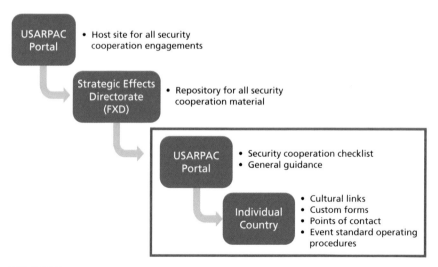

include a link and key search terms for the Center for Army Lessons Learned or Joint Lessons Learned Information System. Additionally, information necessary for the planning of an SC activity may be classified; therefore, a web address for the necessary classified documents should be posted in an easy-to-reference location on each country page.

Improve Access to Cultural Information

The Center for Civil-Military Relations (CCMR) at the Naval Postgraduate School in Monterey, California has been contracted by USARPAC to provide cultural awareness training for participants in large-scale exercises. CCMR provides access to a website where soldiers can do modules on culture and politics of the partner nation where the exercises will occur. CCMR will also schedule a one-week course 45 days before execution for situational training for the leaders of the executing unit. This course is not intended to support small-scale engagements. The training presently does not produce a certificate, but this idea is being considered.

Other potential sources for general, cultural, and political information include the Defense Language Institute and the National Language Service Corps (a nongovernmental organization). Civil affairs units, such as the 84th Civil Affairs Battalion—which is aligned with USARPAC—can also be a source to provide training to units executing events.

Interviewees reported there was a shortage of S9 officers across I Corps units, and the 84th might be a source for meeting this shortfall during SC events.

Standardize Partner-Nation Logistics and Business Guidance in an Accessible Portal

This recommendation is broader than the earlier specific recommendation to create country folders. While both USARPAC and I Corps maintain portals for SC information, interviewees at lower echelons consistently reported that they had trouble accessing those portals. It is beyond the scope of this study to assess whether this is an information technology (IT) problem that requires a technical solution or a process problem in which attempted users are not following the necessary procedures. Nonetheless, given the breadth of individuals and echelons reporting the problem, we speculate that an IT solution may be necessary and recommend that USARPAC further explore the problem of access.

Once access to a portal (or portals) is established, it could be used not only as a repository for country folders, but also for information from units participating in SC events. This could include a "community of interest" roster for each partner nation, training site–specific information, medical and force protection information, cultural customs and courtesies, and partner-nation border control/customs requirements.

Prioritize Major Subordinate Command Staffs If Resources Available

Although IT solutions for the access problems described above should be the first priority if any new funding becomes available, major subordinate command staffs are short on continuity, regional expertise, and SC familiarity. Department of Army civilians with regional and SC expertise would be extremely helpful, especially those with relationships with and close knowledge of USARPAC. However, most units reported that part-time personnel would not be helpful. Instead, new hires might be concentrated at corps and division level, serving as a central resource for all lower echelons, helping to bridge strategic-tactical divide. "Business-practice troubleshooting" (e.g., support with LOAs, passports, etc.), knowledge management, and political/cultural context and relationship-building are candidate functions if additional personnel are made available.

Request a State Department Waiver for Official Passports

The number one challenge mentioned by tactical planners was getting official passports for soldiers' participation in SC events within partner nations that require them. This is currently a time-consuming process that creates frustration at the executing unit headquarters and for deploying soldiers. USARPAC should consider requesting a waiver from the State Department to allow the issuance of official passports without requiring flight schedules and manifests, as the GAO has recommended in the case of USAFRICOM.[2]

Recommendations for USARPAC and I Corps Evaluations: Strategic/Operational-Level Recommendations

Adopt a Theory-of-Change Approach

Building a theory of change approach into the SMS process can help improve the information included in SMS and increase LOE managers' use of SMS in their evaluations. Whether USARPAC or I Corps takes the lead in ownership of evaluation processes, it should use SMS to apply the principles illustrated in Figure 3.4 and the examples in Figures 3.6 and 3.7.

Update Causal Assumptions Included in Theories of Change

In an area such as SC where there is uncertainty about what works, there is often no "right" theory of change. The causal relationships specified in each causal chain will need to be updated as measures evaluating these causal relationships are collected. As is the case with other types of assumptions in a plan, a review/validation of casual assumptions should be conducted periodically as part of the routine assessment process.[3]

Develop MOEs and MOPs That Reflect Objectives and Tasks

MOEs and MOPs should be developed to assess the relevant causal links posited in each SC activity's theory of change. Often, these concepts will not lead easily to quantitative measurement. We expect that this will result in greater reliance on qualitative rather than quantitative metrics. In these cases, planners should specify the questions to ask SMEs or tactical-level executers to gather relevant qualitative indicators. LOE

---

[2] See GAO, 2015, pp. 35–39.

[3] ADRP 5-0 states: "Evaluating includes considering whether the desired conditions have changed, are no longer achievable, or are not achievable through the current operational approach. This is done by continually challenging the key assumptions made when framing the problem. When an assumption is invalidated, then reframing may be in order" (2012, p. 5-3).

managers should be involved in metrics identification process to increase the usefulness of these metrics in the evaluation process.

Evaluate Whether the PMESII Framework Includes the Right Information

In addition to the expected relationships between activities and desired outcomes, theories of change take into account the impact of external factors on activities' likelihood of success. To answer the question "Are there other factors that can affect the expected relationships?" planners and assessors will need access to information on external factors. PMESII's environmental assessment includes many of the factors that might influence the likelihood of success for SC activities. By examining the match between what is currently included in PMESII and what is identified in the theories of change for each SC activity, gaps in PMESII coverage can be identified.

Supplement the Strategic Evaluation Process with Impact Evaluations

Impact evaluations can provide a rigorous assessment for activities that are difficult to assess with other assessment processes and for which it is particularly important to understand how effective USARPAC SC activities are. For SC activities that are strategically important, entail causal relationships that are conceptually uncertain, and are conducted with partners committed to working with the United States, USARPAC could also implement impact evaluations to more rigorously test specific propositions.

Recommendations for USARPAC and I Corps Evaluations: Tactical Evaluations

Use the Available Tools

There are a number of knowledge management solutions that already exist, and as one staff officer noted, "updating the tools that already exist would be a huge benefit."[4] The USARPAC SharePoint portal server and G-TSCMIS are functional but tend to have dated information and in any case are inaccessible by a large number of I Corps and major subordinate command personnel. Fixing the firewall so that these individuals could access the site would be a first step in opening access to a critical AAR repository.

Having dedicated places to put AARs would be another easy fix. These AARs could be uploaded to G-TSCMIS. Additionally, USAR-PAC's FXD-SCP site should have a designated place where AARs are located. Alternately, a link on the initial USARPAC dashboard could provide direction to the USARPAC knowledge management portal, where AARs could be stored. The I Corps portal could be used as a secondary repository, but locating AARs on either the USARPAC or I Corps portals should be backed up by having all AARs placed into G-TSCMIS and the Center for Army Lessons Learned repository. Before an AAR is placed on the Center for Army Lessons Learned site, it should be validated by a knowledge officer, who will ensure the document follows designated naming conventions. Additionally, this officer will tag the document by date, country, and event type so that it is easily searchable. This will allow tactical units to get the information they need quickly. Additionally, information necessary for the planning of an SC activity may be classified; therefore, a web address for the necessary classified documents should be posted in an easy-to-reference location. In every operation order published for an SC event, under the coordinating instructions sections, an additional sentence should be included that requires an AAR to be placed on this site as part of the postmission processes. Finally, a clear standard to maintain this site, and routinely pull outdated or erroneous information, should be enforced.

Senior leader involvement is critical to ensuring that these processes are followed.

Improve Critical Thought and Content

The analysis of AARs provided above shows that there is inadequate critical thought being put into many of them. For mission executors,

---

[4]   Interview with officers in Honolulu, Hawaii, November 4–6, 2015.

there needs to be more structure and thought put into AARs. Higher headquarters, on the other hand, needs to provide more guidance to tactical units about the types of information and critical feedback needed and the standards by which they should evaluate the SC events. Higher headquarters and leaders in general also have a role to play in fostering an institutional culture in which such critical analysis is encouraged.

There are multiple tools, frameworks, and methods concerning AAR methodology, many based on scientific methods of evaluation. Most AAR tools and frameworks are simple and focus on streamlined methods that are appropriate for austere environments. Tools often consist of agendas or checklists that help to guide evaluators, or mission executors, through a sequence of events in the AAR process. Improvements to the AAR framework utilized by most mission executors could yield important benefits to SC activities. One example is root cause analysis, which is a framework often used by government and industry to facilitate understanding and experimentation (see Figure 4.2 for an example). In it, the question "why" is asked iteratively to address the central cause of a problem and understand the way in which a decision-

Figure 4.2
Example of Root Cause Analysis: Bonefish Diagram

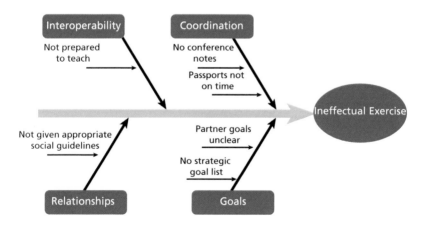

SOURCE: Adapted from Kaoru Ishikawa, *What Is Total Quality Control? The Japanese Way*, translated by David J. Lu, Englewood Cliffs, N.J.: Prentice-Hall, 1985.
RAND RR1920-4.2

maker reached a key decision. The goal is to get to the bottom of why a process works or does not and to build upon positive actions or correct detrimental ones.[5]

Currently, AARs are done primarily at the tactical level for the tactical unit. Therefore, they focus on identifying and fixing tactical issues, not supporting strategic objectives. By involving units in the strategic evaluation process for an SC activity, they may become more invested in the strategic results of that action as they become more aware of their role in achieving theater goals and report on their success in that role to others.

To help AARs be more useful, they need to reflect more of the root problems of an event. In general, negative comments are a rarity in AARs, and there appears to be considerable reluctance to share negative feedback. The most likely reason for this is that units do not want to provide negative feedback in an AAR because they feel their higher headquarters will question the unit's performance. The assumption appears to be that a mission executor will be judged harshly if an event is said to have not gone well. Senior leaders have a critical role to play in supporting an environment that welcomes critical feedback and understands failures to achieve SC goals as the end result of a broader process, not the shortcomings of any one leader.

Create New Sites or Make Better Use of Existing Ones

Not all information needs to be hung on a restricted access website, and many SC professionals, tactical and strategic, would benefit from access to an unclassified portal on a milSuite/milBook site. A community of interest with information—such as a country's history, culture, and import/customs requirements—could be created for each country in the USPACOM AOR that would serve as an additional repository for information, and anyone with a Common Access Card could access this site.

---

[5]   This section drew on Bill Gelfeld and Christopher Nelson's unpublished RAND research. We are grateful for their insights into AARs and evaluation.

Create a Template for Information on Partner-Nation Strengths and Weaknesses

In order to maximize the usefulness of AARs for providing information on foreign security forces and the United States' ability to partner with them, AARs would ideally follow a common template. The precise content of this template should be determined by USARPAC and tactical units in cooperation with one another, but individual fields might include capabilities of a partner-nation unit; types of operations in which it has previously participated; information on the terrain for the event; and known interoperability issues. Setting up this type of repository would not necessarily be a difficult task, claimed one USARPAC officer, but ensuring that the information is up to date would require senior leadership involvement. The same officer said that the information does not need to be perfect, and would not have to include every detail and date. However, a repository like this would at least give tactical planners "close to the right answer."[6]

Use New Products "Evaluation Toolkit"

To facilitate coordination among the many stakeholders in this AOR, we have provided a number of products and templates, which we have collectively termed the "Evaluation Toolkit." USARPAC and other commands may decide to adopt them as they are, to modify them, or to not use them at all, but they are intended at least to facilitate discussion about what such common tools and templates might look like. The Evaluation Toolkit is designed to help bridge the gap between mission executors and planners. Included in these documents are a series of AAR templates that are designed specifically for SC events from the small team level to larger brigade-sized elements. Appendixes B and C are AAR templates designed to be a used by small team missions to provide feedback on information that is important to planners and evaluators at higher headquarters; Appendix B is an abbreviated template to be used for units that are time constrained, and Appendix C is a more comprehensive template. Appendix D is an AAR tem-

---

[6] Information in this paragraph was drawn from interviews with officers in Honolulu, Hawaii, November 4–6, 2015.

plate designed for larger SC events, such as missions that are part of Pacific Pathways. All of the templates have an SC and evaluation focus. They are designed to capture information on a partner nation's security forces, report on specific tasks, and provide critical insight into mission execution.

Appendix E is the evaluation scorecard. It is a tool designed to jointly assess U.S. and partner nation–executed training. U.S. units have methods to assess training and unit-level proficiency through tools such as mission-essential task lists, training outlines and evaluations, and other grading rubrics. The intent of this tool is to help apply these methods, which are already familiar to Army personnel, to partner-nation units.

Ideally, the toolkit will be housed within the USARPAC portal under the Security Cooperation Policy Division and will include the abovementioned documents. To facilitate access to these documents, they should be tagged by date, activity type, unit executor and partner-nation unit, and could be located in an AAR folder on the portal page.

Taken together, these recommendations offer opportunities to improve the flow of guidance and information between strategic and tactical levels, better linking specific SC activities to the strategic goals that they are intended to support.

AAR Coding Scheme

In each instance, the issue should provide quantifiable data, but we should also extract important quotes or other qualitative data to convey nuances that simple counts will not provide (and especially any suggestions for improvements).[1]

Background/Context

1. Title of Event (or AAR for multiple events or programs)

2. Brief Description of Event Objectives

3. Location(s): Where did the SC event occur?

4. Dates: When did the SC event occur? (date started, date ended)

5. Duration: How long did the SC event last? (days)

6. Type of Activity: SME exchange, command post exercise, multilateral exercise, staff planning, etc.

7. Scale of Activity: # of participants (if available) and unit size (squad or smaller, platoon, company, battalion, brigade, higher headquarters?)

8. Type of U.S. and partner units involved:

---

[1] This template was developed from the following sources: Army Regulation 11-33, 2006; a selection of USARPAC/I Corps AARs; and Chairman of the Joint Chiefs of Staff Instruction 3150.25C, 2007. For an overview of the Marine Corps Lessons Learned Program, see U.S. Marines, "Marine Corps Lessons Learned Program (MCLLP) and the Marine Corps Center for Lessons Learned (MCCLL)," February 2, 2008. The materials on formats and lessons developed through this system are not available to the public.

- **Type of U.S. Unit Involved:** Staff, 25 Infantry Division, 8th Theater Sustainment Command, brigade combat team, Representatives of Defense Threat Reduction Activity, USARPAC, etc.
- **Unit Type code:** Platoon, battalion, brigade, small team, very small team
- **Type of Partner Units Involved:** country unit and name

9. Status of U.S. Forces (active component: temporary duty, temporary change of station/reserve component: overseas deployment training, mobilization)

10. Reporting Requirements: What higher headquarters did the unit report to during the event(s)? Battalion, brigade, division, corps, ASCC, geographic combatant command?

11. Type of AAR: Storyboard, AAR by SME exchange lead officer, AAR from brigade combat team S3, AAR from event coordinator

Strategic Planning

1. Sustainability of Capabilities

- **Positive:** Processes to ensure that Building Partner Capacity gains made by partner forces would be sustained were strong or sufficient.
- **Negative:** Processes to ensure that Building Partner Capacity gains made by partner forces would be sustained were weak or entirely lacking.
- **Neutral:** Ambiguous references to SC events' ability to sustain Building Partner Capacity gains.
- **No mention**

2. Sustainability of Relationships

- **Positive:** Processes to ensure that relationships made with partner forces would be sustained were strong or sufficient.
- **Negative:** Processes to ensure that relationships made with partner forces would be sustained were weak or entirely lacking.

- **Neutral:** Ambiguous references to SC events' ability to sustain relationships.
- **No mention**

Tactical Planning

1. "Nesting" Within Higher-Level Objectives

- **Positive:** SC activities clearly demonstrated relationship to strategic objectives.
- **Negative:** SC activities lacked any demonstrable relationship to strategic objectives.
- **Neutral:** Ambiguous references to SC events' relationship to strategic objectives.
- **No mention**

2. Availability of Information Required for Tactical Planning

- **Positive:** Units involved in SC had sufficient knowledge of partner capabilities and other environmental factors to successfully plan for the SC event.
- **Negative:** Units involved in SC lacked sufficient knowledge of partner capabilities and other environmental factors to successfully plan for the SC event.
- **Neutral:** Ambiguous references to information required for tactical planning.
- **No mention**

Coordination

1. Harmonization of Global Response and TSC Missions

- **Positive:** Conflicts between the deploying unit's global response and TSC missions were manageable.

- **Negative:** Conflicts between the deploying unit's global response and TSC missions posed considerable problems for unit planning and preparation.
- **Neutral:** Ambiguous references to conflicts between the deploying unit's global response and TSC missions.
- **No mention**

2. Timeliness of Mission Assignment: When was unit notified of event? (Days in advance)

- **Positive:** Units conducting SC received their assigned missions with sufficient time to prepare.
- **Negative:** Units conducting SC received their assigned missions with insufficient time to prepare.
- **Neutral:** Ambiguous references to whether units conducting SC had sufficient time to prepare.
- **No mention**

3. Coordination with Other U.S. Military Units—Awareness of Related Activities

- **Positive:** Deploying units were aware of related activities of other U.S. units in the same country or region and had the opportunity to benefit from their insights or contacts.
- **Negative:** Deploying units were not aware of related activities of other U.S. units in the same country or region and/or did not have the opportunity to benefit from their insights or contacts.
- **Neutral:** Ambiguous references to awareness of related U.S. SC activities.
- **No mention**

4. Coordination with Host Nation

- **Positive:** The requisite contacts and procedures were in place to ensure the SC event could proceed without major incident or delay.

- **Negative:** The requisite contacts and procedures were not in place, causing negative incidents or substantial delays.
- **Neutral:** Ambiguous references to coordination with host nation.
- **No mention**

Preparations

1. Regional Familiarity—Establishing Appropriate Expectations

- **Positive:** U.S. forces had appropriate expectations about how much partner forces could learn or how quickly they could achieve specified goals of the SC event.
- **Negative:** U.S. forces had overly ambitious expectations about how much partner forces could learn or how quickly they could achieve specified goals of the SC event.
- **Neutral:** Ambiguous references to the appropriateness of U.S. forces' expectations.
- **No mention**

2. Regional Familiarity—Inculcating Respect for Partner Nation and Its Forces

- **Positive:** U.S. forces demonstrated an appropriate attitude toward the partner nation or foreign security forces (FSF).
- **Negative:** U.S. forces frequently demonstrated a patronizing or disrespectful attitude toward the partner nation or FSF.
- **Neutral:** Ambiguous references to the appropriateness of U.S. forces' demonstrated attitudes.
- **No mention**

3. Partnering Skills

- **Positive:** Preparation for SC events included adequate time dedicated to learning partnering skills.
- **Negative:** Preparation for SC events should include more time dedicated to learning partnering skills and/or culminating train-

ing event exercises or other capstone events should place greater emphasis on such skills.

- **Neutral:** Ambiguous references to the appropriateness of U.S. forces' preparation time dedicated to learning partnering skills.
- **No mention**

4. Task Organization

- **Positive:** Unit is adequately sized and organized to achieve its mission and to meet the partner nations' demands; a desirable partnership ratio is achieved.
- **Negative:** Unit is not capable of achieving the desired partnership ratio; it lacks a critical enabler capability required by the mission or desired by the partner.
- **Neutral:** Ambiguous references to the size and/or organization of U.S. forces.
- **No mention**

5. Predeployment Training

- **Positive:** Predeployment culminating training event adequately simulated, if not replicated, deployed mission requirements and environment.
- **Negative:** Predeployment culminating training event unrelated to deployed mission requirements or environment. (For example, a decisive action training environment counter-terrorism committee rotation when the requirement is to conduct security force assistance; a national training center rotation in the desert when the unit will be operating in the jungle, etc.)
- **Neutral:** Ambiguous references to U.S. forces' predeployment training activities
- **No mention**

Personnel Requirements

1. Foreign Language Capabilities

- **Positive:** U.S. forces conducting SC activities possessed adequate foreign language competence, either through the foreign-language competence of U.S. forces, the services of interpreters, or the English-language competence of partner forces.
- **Negative:** U.S. forces conducting SC activities would have benefited significantly from greater foreign language competence, either among U.S. military personnel or through contractors supplied by the U.S. government.
- **Neutral:** Ambiguous references to foreign language capabilities.
- **No mention**

2. Continuity in Relationships

- **Positive:** Personnel continuity in critical U.S. SC positions was adequate.
- **Negative:** Partnering activities should ideally be coordinated or facilitated by someone with greater continuity in their position than possessed by the U.S. personnel responsible for the event; many aspects of partnership require mutual understanding and trust that does not develop quickly, and many partner-nation personnel find the constant turnover among U.S. military personnel disorienting.
- **Neutral:** Ambiguous references to continuity in relationships.
- **No mention**

3. Selection of Personnel for Key Roles in SC

- **Positive:** Selection of personnel for key roles in the conduct of SC was appropriate and procedures in place for this selection process were adequate.
- **Negative:** Not everyone is suited by disposition and/or prior experience to play a critical role in SC; personnel should be selected from participating U.S. units on the basis of a more formal selec-

tion procedure than is currently used in order to ensure the most appropriate personnel play key roles.

- **Neutral:** Ambiguous references to personnel selection.
- **No mention**

Evaluation

1. Need for More Rigorous Evaluations: Were MOPs and MOEs listed in the AAR? If yes, what were they?

- **Positive:** Existing evaluation mechanisms are adequate for evaluating the success of SC activities.
- **Negative:** Existing evaluation mechanisms are inadequate for evaluating the success of SC activities; more formal and rigorous evaluation mechanisms are needed.
- **Neutral:** Ambiguous references to evaluations.
- **No mention**

2. Self-Critical Evaluation

- **Positive (Self-critical):** This subject gets after the "why" of SC activities. To be coded self-critical the AAR needed to address specific methods to improve planning, execution, use or validity of the mission and future activities AAR was analytical and addressed specific methods to improve the SC activity.
- **Negative (Not Self-critical):** The AAR did not address specific methods to improve planning, execution, mission validity and future activities. The AAR was not analytical and did not address specific methods to improve SC activity; comments could have addressed specific methods to improve the SC activity.
- **Neutral (Semicritical):** The AAR addressed a combination of planning, execution, mission validity and follow on activities. It did not address all of these items in an analytical manner. Alternately, it avoided specific methods to improve SC activities.
- **No mention**

3. Evaluation/Reporting System Used

- **Positive:** Evaluation/Reporting system was used and thoroughly robust to provide qualitative and quantitative data.
- **Negative:** Evaluation/Reporting system was insufficient to provide qualitative and quantitative data.
- **Neutral:** Evaluation/Reporting system was adequate to provide some qualitative and quantitative data.
- **No mention**

Provide Information for Future Missions

1. Addresses FSF Capabilities

- **Positive:** FSF capabilities were addressed in a categorically structured manner. Useful information was provided on the partner-nation unit, either positive or critical in nature.
- **Negative:** Information on FSF is necessary to plan for and execute specific training to partner-nation units. Capabilities were described in a manner that is irrelevant for follow on missions or provided no additional insight into their capabilities.
- **Neutral:** Ambiguous references to FSF capabilities. Capabilities were referenced, but references only addressed part of the training and were only moderately helpful for future activities.
- **No mention**

2. Logistics

- **Positive:** Addressed specific logistical issues, classes of supply, and how to improve them.
- **Negative:** Logistical process in place was insufficient. The mission lacked sustainment resources.
- **Neutral:** Ambiguous references that do not contribute to a better-resourced mission.
- **No mention**

3. Administration

- **Positive:** Adequate administration processes were in place and discussed in the AAR. Follow on action would be easy to repeat or build upon.
- **Negative:** Inadequate administration processes were in place, which lead to a delayed, impaired, or cancelled event.
- **Neutral:** Administration processes were addressed, with no method of improvement or reference to how they impacted the event.
- **No mention**

4. Training

- **Positive:** Specific training conducted during the event was at the appropriate level for partner-nation forces. Training was described and provided key insights into how U.S. forces should engage with the partner nation in the future.
- **Negative:** Training was not at the appropriate level for either U.S. forces or partner-nation forces; the training was either too basic or too advanced for partner-nation forces.
- **Neutral:** Ambiguous references to training events, some training was conducted but it was unclear what training, how much or the quality of the training. Unclear what follow on actions should be.
- **No mention**

5. Communications

- **Positive:** Communications systems were in place and utilized during the event, information flowed freely.
- **Negative:** Ineffective or inappropriate communication systems. Information was stove-piped and communication was hindered.
- **Neutral:** Some communication systems were in place and utilized, not entirely effective.
- **No mention**

6. Equipment

- **Positive:** Mission-specific references to equipment were addressed. Included type of equipment, issues resulting from that equipment and methods to address the issues.
- **Negative:** Ineffective or inappropriate equipment systems in place for the training.
- **Neutral:** Ambiguous references equipment used during the event.
- **No mention**

7. Mission Conducted

- **Positive:** The planned mission was conducted.
- **Negative:** The mission was not conducted. No basis for follow on missions provided.
- **Neutral:** Phases of the mission were conducted, but not completely, and some phases of the operation did not occur.
- **No mention**

8. Strategic Communication

- **Positive:** Strategic communication guidance was planned for and utilized during the event.
- **Negative:** Strategic communication guidance was not planned for or conducted.
- **Neutral:** Strategic guidance was planned for but not adequately executed. It did not support all of the training activities that occurred.
- **No mention**

AAR Template for Small-Scale SC Event (Abbreviated)

Exercise Summary

- Mission:
- U.S. unit Mission Essential Task List tasks trained:
- Key U.S. tasks or LOEs:
- Phases of operation/agenda: (Planning, Advanced Echelon, daily activity)
- USARPAC objectives addressed:

Unit Information

- Unit(s):
- Number of personnel:
- Mission title and G-TSCMIS Number:
- Location of event:
- Dates of event:
- Mission commander and/or action officer:
- Country team point of contact:

Partner-Nation Unit

- Unit(s):
- Number of personnel:
- Names, positions, and contact information of key leaders:
- Dates attended:

- Key tasks trained and rating of partner nation (untrained, proficient, trained):

Key Question Section

- Describe what capabilities were achieved—compare the start vs. the end of training.
- Key interoperability gaps—what appeared to be the most important challenges to interoperability between partner-nation and U.S. forces?
- How did you assess training? Did you have Training and Evaluation Outlines, MOEs, and MOPs? Were they provided to you by headquarters? How would evaluate the event better next time?
- How did the event contribute to building partner capacity, maintaining access, building relationships, country objectives? What would have been more effective?
- Would you recommend this mission in the future? What would you change? What types of activities worked well, what did not?

Enclosures (if applicable)

- concept of operations
- agenda
- map
- photographs
- attendance roster
- key leader interview

AAR Template for Small-Scale SC Event

Exercise Summary

- Mission:
- U.S. unit Mission Essential Task List tasks trained:
- Key U.S. tasks or LOEs:
- Phases of operation/agenda: (Planning, Advanced Echelon, daily activity)
- USARPAC Objectives addressed:

Unit Information

- Unit(s):
- Number of personnel:
- Mission title and G-TSCMIS Number:
- Location of event:
- Dates of event:
- Mission commander and/or action officer:
- Country team point of contact:

Partner-Nation Unit

- Unit(s):
- Number of personnel:
- Names, positions, and contact information of key leaders:
- Dates attended:

- Key tasks trained and rating of partner nation (untrained, proficient, trained):

Key Question Section

- Describe what capabilities were achieved—compare the start vs. the end of training.
- Key interoperability gaps—what appeared to be the most important challenges to interoperability between partner-nation and U.S. forces?
- How did you assess training? Did you have Training and Evaluation Outlines, MOEs and MOPs? Were they provided to you by headquarters? How would evaluate the event better next time?
- How did the event contribute to building partner capacity, maintaining access, building relationships, country objectives? What would have been more effective?
- Would you recommend this mission in the future? What would you change? What types of activities worked well, what did not?

Planning

Use this area to discuss pre-event information (unit notification, preparation and expectations for event, understanding of task and purpose, understanding of requirements, usefulness of OPORD instructions, overall planning requirements and necessary information and coordination opportunities, guidance for priorities, schedule of working groups, time for post-deployment software support activities, and higher element support).

- Discussion:
- Insight/Lesson:

Administration/Logistics

Use this area to discuss requirements for mission execution, passports, Defense Travel System, Training Course Completions Report, coordination with country team, shipment of mission essential material, sustainment, lodging, and service support issues.

- Issue:
- Discussion:
- Insight/Lesson:

Operation/Execution

Use this area to discuss how well the event occurred, the phase of the operation, daily activities, and training conducted.

- Issue:
- Discussion:
- Insight/Lesson:

Communication

Use this area to discuss the communication plan, how it was established with the partner nation, how well it was executed, and which systems were utilized. Address strategic communication—was the event covered by newspapers, social media, radio? Was a joint partner-nation and U.S. statement issued? Were foreign dignitaries present? If so, who? How did we engage with them? Was it appropriate?

- Issue:
- Discussion:
- Insight/Lesson:

Financial Transaction Summary

(Use this section to address funding for the event.)

- Requested/Approved:
- Committed/Executed:
- Summary:

Conclusion/Future Recommendations/Way Ahead

How could this event be improved in the future? What went well? What did not go well? What lessons did you learn that should be shared with other units preparing for other SC events? What do you wish you knew from the start?

Enclosures (if applicable)

- concept of operations
- agenda
- map
- photographs
- attendance roster
- key leader interview

AAR Template for Large-Scale SC Event

Report cover page

- classification
- preparing headquarters or organization
- location of report preparation
- date of preparation
- period covered (date to date)

Preface or foreword signed by the commander

Table of contents (chronological/operational phases, then by warfighting function)

Executive summary and chronology of significant events:

- Briefly summarize operations for all phases; include key dates for each phase starting with predeployment, deployment, and ending with redeployment.
- Summarize task organization.
- Summarize key trained Mission Essential Task List.
- Describe partner-nation tasks.
- What capabilities were achieved?
- Where did the partner-nation force begin? Where did they end?
- Summarize key lessons learned.
- Summarize recommendations.

Detailed task organization (include any significant changes and dates as appropriate)

- organizational diagrams, including attached units, elements, and named task forces, including enablers and clearance authorities
- highlight any significant task organizational challenges (command and support relationships) and how they were mitigated
- effective dates of task organization to include all attached, operationally controlled units and individuals, contractors, partnernation forces, and liaison officers

Predeployment phase with dates

- Unit's training focus
  - Describe the training plan.
  - Was the unit able to train as a combined arms team with all deploying assets participating? Was it certified?
  - What assets outside the unit were used to support training?
- What were the key and essential areas trained?
- Describe what simulation systems (such as live, virtual, constructive, and gaming) were instrumental in training success.
- Discuss lessons learned during predeployment operations. What was planned but not executed?
- Discuss logistics and personnel shortages.
- Discuss planning for rear detachment operations.
- Describe any major shifts in personnel or manning.
- What were the significant predeployment training lessons learned?
  - issues
  - discussions
  - insights/lessons
- What were the significant gaps identified in leader development or proficiency?
- Deployment and reception, staging, onward movement, and integration (RSOI) with dates:
  - Summarize deployment and RSOI operations—including arrival in partner nation.

- Discuss what portions of the RSOI process went as planned and what worked.
- What were the shortcomings and delays in the RSOI?

Operations phase with dates

- Summarize tactical and nontactical operations (sometimes beneficial to do this by staff element or warfighting function).
- Include unit participation in named operations.
- List of key OPORDs and FRAGOs.
- Discuss operations phases by event (sometimes beneficial to address by warfighting function).
- Discuss any mission command challenges.

Redeployment activities with dates

- Summarize redeployment activities and highlight planning guidance either developed or received from higher headquarters.
- Redeployment timeline
- List of critical losses, personnel, equipment, and information

Postdeployment activities

- Discuss combat stress planning and reintegration activities.
- Discuss plans and priorities used in reconstituting and resetting the unit.
- Place this AAR and other documents on I-Corps SC portal.
  - Include a staff or section point of contact for follow-up coordination.
  - Include classification, titles, and distribution or disposition of reports.

Appendixes (as appropriate)

- list of each named operation or major event with dates.
- applicable maps
- photographs

- copies of key OPORDs and FRAGOs
- particularly useful tactics, techniques, or procedures or unit products developed
- predeployment site survey information
- rear detachment operations
- unit daily journals
- key leader interviews

Security Cooperation Training Scorecard

Purpose: To measure the impact of training on both U.S. and partner-nation units. This scorecard (see Table E.1 for a sample) is to be used as an assessment and instructional tool. The U.S. and partner-nation unit commanders input the Mission Essential Tasks to be trained during the event side-by-side, prior to the beginning of training. Each commander would fill out the tasks to be accomplished during the event for their respective units. At the end of the training, the U.S. and partner-nation commanders will assess the level, quality and effect of the training on their respective units. Each unit commander will input into the scorecard (U)ntrained, (P)roficient, or (T)rained.

Description/rationale: The training scorecard measures positive changes in unit readiness directly resulting from the training activities completed during the event. Both U.S. and partner-nation leadership will benefit from the exercise of filling in the scorecard. The scorecard is designed to facilitate dialogue between unit commanders and their staff.

Data Source and Collection Method

The scorecard's unit of measurement is at the individual unit level. SC unit executors should complete a single score card for each training event or upon the completion of a large exercise. SC unit executors should work in collaboration with partner-nation units to complete the scorecard.

Table E.1
Training Score Card

Training Objective (Mission Essential Task, Army Tactical Task)	U.S. Unit: Before-Event Assessment (U, P, T)	U.S. Unit: After-Event Assessment (U, P, T)	Partner-Nation Unit: Before-Event Assessment (U, P, T)	Partner-Nation Unit: After-Event Assessment (U, P, T)
1. Conduct Populace and Resource Control— Army Tactical Task 7.3.3.4	P	P+	U	U+
2.				
3.				
4.				
5.				

Instructions: There are two primary methods to input information onto the scorecard, based on likely conditions that U.S. personnel will encounter when conducting an SC event.

• Before mission execution, the U.S. unit commander and partner-nation unit commander jointly provide training objectives to be accomplished during the event for their respective units. Both commanders will discuss their training objectives, currently level of proficiency and what they hope to get from the training. Commanders will then complete the columns "U.S./ Partner-Nation Before-Event Assessment" based on their current assessment for each activity. The units will then execute the training. Upon completion of the training, the commanders will again get together and have a discussion on the quality of the training conducted, whether their training objectives were met and how their unit has improved. They will then fill out the columns "U.S./Partner-Nation After-Event Assessment" on the tasks that were trained during the event.

- In the event that the partner-nation commander is unable or unwilling to provide input into the scorecard, the U.S. commander should complete the "U.S./Partner-Nation Before-Event Assessment" to the best of their ability. Upon the completion of the event, the U.S. commander will complete both the "U.S./Partner-Nation After-Event Assessment" portions of the scorecard.
- The U.S. commander may disagree with the partner-nation assessment. In this instance, a detailed explanation should be provided describing, by task, the discrepancies.

References

ADRP—*See* Army Doctrine Reference Publication.

Army Doctrine Publication 3-0, *Unified Land Operations*, Washington, D.C.: Headquarters, Department of the Army, October 2011.

Army Regulation 11-33, *Army Lessons Learned Program*, Washington, D.C.: Headquarters, Department of the Army, October 17, 2006.

Army Doctrine Reference Publication 5-0, *The Operations Process*, Washington, D.C.: Headquarters, Department of the Army, May 17, 2012.

Army Regulation 11-33, *Army Lessons Learned Program (ALLP)*, Washington, D.C.: Headquarters, Department of the Army, draft, undated. Not available to the public.

Bachl, Chris, and Molly Kihara, "USARPAC Metrics in Support of Campaign Assessment," presentation to USARPAC, March 12, 2014.

Bennett, Benjamin A., *Integrating Landpower in the Indo–Asia–Pacific Through 2020: Analysis of a Theater Army Campaign Design*, Arlington, Va.: Association of the United States Army, Institute of Land Warfare, The Land Warfare Papers No. 107, May 2015a. As of March 1, 2016:
https://www.ausa.org/publications/integrating-landpower-indo%E2%80%93asia%E2%80%93pacific-through-2020-analysis-theater-army-campaign

Bennett, Benjamin A., *Integrating Landpower in the Indo–Asia–Pacific Through 2020: Analysis of a Theater Army Campaign Design*, briefing to the Association of the United States Army National Convention, October 14, 2015b. As of March 1, 2016:
http://am2015.ausa.org/wp-content/uploads/2015/10/BenjaminBennett.pdf

Brooks, Vincent K., "U.S. Army Pacific and the Pacific Rebalance," *Army*, October 2013, pp. 121–126.

Cameron, Drew B., Annette N. Brown, Anjini Mishra, Mario Picon, Hisham Esper, Flor Calvo, and Katia Peterson, *Evidence for Peacebuilding: An Evidence Gap Map*, New Delhi: International Initiative for Impact Evaluation, Evidence Gap Map Report 1, April 2015.

Center for Army Lessons Learned, "Bulletin 16-09: Security Cooperation: Lessons and Best Practices," March 2016.

Chairman of the Joint Chiefs of Staff, *CJCS Guide to the Chairman's Readiness System*, Washington, D.C.: Office of the Chairman of the Joint Chiefs of Staff, CJCS Guide 3401D, November 15, 2010.

Chairman of the Joint Chiefs of Staff, "Lessons Learned Collection Efforts for Military Operations," Washington, D.C., Memorandum for Chiefs of the Military Services, CM-0028-14, February 4, 2014. As of March 25, 2017: http://www.public.navy.mil/bupers-npc/reference/messages/Documents/ NAVADMINS/NAV2014/NAV14075.txt

Chairman of the Joint Chiefs of Staff Instruction 3150.25C, "Joint Lessons Learned Program," Washington, D.C.: Office of the Chairman of the Joint Chiefs of Staff, 2007.

Committee on Evaluation of USAID Democracy Assistance Programs, *Improving Democracy Assistance: Building Knowledge Through Evaluations and Research*, Washington, D.C.: National Academies Press, 2008.

Department of the Army Pamphlet 11-31, *Army Security Cooperation Handbook*, Washington, D.C.: Headquarters, Department of the Army, February 6, 2015.

Field Manual 3-07.1, *Security Force Assistance*, Washington, D.C.: Headquarters, Department of the Army, May 1, 2009.

Field Manual 3-22, *Army Support to Security Cooperation*, Washington, D.C.: Headquarters, Department of the Army, January 2013.

Field Manual 6-0, *Commander and Staff Organization and Operations*, Washington, D.C.: Headquarters, Department of the Army, May 2014.

FM—*See* Field Manual.

Fowlie, Meredith, Michael Greenstone, and Catherine Wolfram, "Are the Non-monetary Costs of Energy Efficiency Investments Large? Understanding Low Take-Up of a Free Energy Efficiency Program," *American Economic Review*, Vol. 105, No. 5, 2015, pp. 201–204.

Gelfeld, Bill, and Christopher Nelson, Santa Monica, Calif.: RAND Corporation, unpublished manuscript.

Halachmi, Arie, "Performance Measurement Is Only One Way of Managing Performance," *International Journal of Productivity and Performance Management*, Vol. 54, No. 7, 2005, pp. 502–516.

"I Corps Orders Writing, Staffing and Publishing," I Corps G3 Memorandum, January 22, 2013.

Ishikawa, Kaoru, *What Is Total Quality Control? The Japanese Way*, translated by David J. Lu, Englewood Cliffs, N.J.: Prentice-Hall, 1985.

Joint Publication 1-02, *DOD Dictionary of Military and Associated Terms*, Washington, D.C.: Department of Defense, November 8, 2010 (amended February 15, 2016). As of February 29, 2016:
http://www.dtic.mil/doctrine/new_pubs/jp1_02.pdf

Joint Publication 3-0, *Joint Operations*, Washington, D.C.: Chairman of the Joint Chiefs of Staff, August 11, 2011.

Joint Publication 5-0, *Joint Operation Planning*, Washington, D.C., Joint Chiefs of Staff, August 11, 2011.

JP—*See* Joint Publication.

Koleros, Andrew, "Using Theories of Change for Monitoring, Evaluation and Learning," paper presented at Overseas Development Institute's Conference on Theories of Change in International Development, April 7, 2015. As of January 2017:
https://www.odi.org/sites/odi.org.uk/files/odi-assets/events-presentations/1709.pdf

Mayne, John, and Nancy Johnson, "Using Theories of Change in the CGIAR Research Program on Agriculture for Nutrition and Health," *Evaluation*, Vol. 21, No. 4, 2015, pp. 407–428.

McHugh, John M., and Raymond T. Odierno, "Army Strategic Guidance for Security Cooperation: An Enduring Mission for Prevent, Shape, Win," Department of the Army, August 2014.

McNerney, Michael, Angela O'Mahony, Thomas S. Szayna, Derek Eaton, Caroline Baxter, Colin P. Clarke, Emma Cutrufello, Michael McGee, Heather Peterson, Leslie Adrienne Payne, and Calin Trenkov-Wermuth, *Assessing Security Cooperation as a Preventive Tool*, Santa Monica, Calif.: RAND Corporation, RR-350-A, 2014. As of June 22, 2017:
http://www.rand.org/pubs/research_reports/RR350.html

Moynihan, Donald P., *The Dynamics of Performance Management: Constructing Information and Reform*, Washington, D.C.: Georgetown University Press, Public Management and Change Series, 2008.

Office of the Deputy Assistant Secretary of Defense for Plans, *Theater Campaign Planning: Planners' Handbook*, Washington, D.C.: Office of the Deputy Assistant Secretary of Defense for Plans, February 2012.

Osburg, Jan, Christopher Paul, Lisa Saum-Manning, Dan Madden, and Leslie Adrienne Payne, *Assessing Locally Focused Stability Operations*, Santa Monica, Calif.: RAND Corporation, RR-387-A, 2014. As of March 15, 2017:
http://www.rand.org/pubs/research_reports/RR387.html

Paul, Christopher, Colin P. Clarke, Beth Grill, Stephanie Young, Jennifer D. P. Moroney, Joe Hogler, and Christine Leah, *What Works Best When Building Partner Capacity and Under What Circumstances?* Santa Monica, Calif.: RAND Corporation, MG-1253/1-OSD, 2013. As of June 22, 2017:
http://www.rand.org/pubs/monographs/MG1253z1.html

Radin, Andrew, "The Misunderstood Lessons of Bosnia for Syria," *Washington Quarterly*, Vol. 37, No. 4, 2015, pp. 55–69.

U.S. Army Pacific, "USARPAC: One Team," website, undated. As of March 4, 2016:
http://www.usarpac.army.mil/misvis.asp

U.S. Army Pacific, "U.S. Army Pacific Response to GAO Questions (GAO 100187 Review of the Army's Pacific Pathways Program, Questions for USARPAC Draft Version 3)," 2015, p. 9.

U.S. Army Pacific, "USARPAC Theater Environmental Analysis (Using the PMESII Model)," PowerPoint presentation, limited distribution, April 2015.

U.S. Army Pacific, "Pacific Pathways 2016: U.S. Army Pacific Readiness and the Strategic Rebalance," pamphlet, 2016. As of January 13, 2017:
http://www.usarpac.army.mil/pdfs/Pacific%20Pathways%202016%20Tri-fold.pdf

U.S. Army Training and Doctrine Command, Training and Doctrine Command Pamphlet 525-5-500, *Commander's Appreciation and Campaign Design,* Fort Monroe, Virginia, January 28, 2008. As of June 22, 2017:
http://www.tradoc.army.mil/tpubs/pams/p525-5-500.pdf

U.S. Government Accountability Office, "Regionally Aligned Forces: DoD Could Enhance Army Brigades' Efforts in Africa by Improving Activity Coordination and Mission-Specific Preparation," GAO-15-568, August 2015. As of March 1, 2016:
http://www.gao.gov/assets/680/672157.pdf

U.S. Marines, "Marine Corps Lessons Learned Program (MCLLP) and the Marine Corps Center for Lessons Learned (MCCLL)," February 2, 2008. As of July 21, 2017:
http://www.marines.mil/News/Messages/Messages-Display/Article/893717/marine-corps-lessons-learned-program-mcllp-and-the-marine-corps-center-for-less/

White House Office of the Press Secretary, "Remarks by President Obama to the Australian Parliament," November 17, 2011.